Brain Scans

James Aitchison

SCOTTISH CONTEMPORARY POETS SERIES

SCOTTISH CULTURAL PRESS

First published 1998
by Scottish Cultural Press
Unit 14, Leith Walk Business Centre
130 Leith Walk
Edinburgh EH6 5DT
Tel: 0131 555 5950 • Fax: 0131 555 5018
e-mail: scp@sol.co.uk

British Library Cataloguing in Publication Data
A catalogue for this book is available from the British Library

ISBN: 1 898218 91 9

The publisher acknowledges subsidy from the Scottish Arts Council
towards the publication of this book

THE SCOTTISH ARTS COUNCIL

Printed and bound by
Cromwell Press Ltd, Trowbridge, Wiltshire

Scottish Contemporary Poets Series
(for further details of this series please contact the publishers)

Contents

James Aitchison was born in Stirlingshire and educated at the Universities of Glasgow and Strathclyde, where he was awarded a doctorate for research on Edwin Muir. He worked as a publicity copywriter, an information officer and a lecturer in English language. His literary journalism has appeared in *The Scotsman,* the *Glasgow Herald, Lines Review* and other journals.

By the same author:

Poetry
Sounds Before Sleep
Spheres
Second Nature

Criticism
The Golden Harvester: The Vision of Edwin Muir

Edited, with Alexander Scott
New Writing Scotland, vols. 1, 2, 3

Reference
Cassell Guide to Written English
Cassell Dictionary of English Grammar

Acknowledgements

'Canada: Awakening The Trees' won the Canadian Writing Wilderness poetry competition in 1992 and appeared in *The Fiddlehead*. 'Neurological Rounds' was published in *Gairfish;* 'Edward Thomas: Embarkation Leave, December 1916' was published in *Poetry Wales*.

Other poems in this collection appeared in *Cencrastus, Cumbria, The Dark Horse, Lines Review, The New Criterion, New Writing Scotland, NorthWords, Orbis, Poesie Europe, The Scotsman, Southfields,* and the *Thomas Hardy Journal*.

I am grateful to the editors of these journals and to W N Herbert, Richard Price and George Szirtes for their helpful comments on earlier versions of some poems in the collection.

The publisher acknowledges an award from the Deric Bolton Poetry Trust towards the publication of this volume

1 Brain Scans

Brain Scans

Words
for Richard Price

Words... words... words... words... Dictionaries fail.
They haven't got the accent or detail
I'm looking for. Perhaps the thing that stirred
can't be decoded by the written word.
Perhaps language creates as it destroys,
corrupting signals into random noise.
But I keep looking, trying to express
in words the nature of the wordlessness
that ripples through forgotten and half-known
channels of the memory's lexicon
where language is inchoate, and the brain
must discover how to write again
in words without a future or a past,
as if this were my first poem and my last.

Hysteria

You hated, and your hatred scraped for forty years
of poetry from your tongue. Rage stripped your face
of its thin layer of humanity.

You panicked. Your brain was so full of fear
there was nowhere left for mind; there was no space
for consciousness to keep its tenancy.

You felt so sad you couldn't resist despair's
corrupt, voluptuous embrace
of thought and language, self and sanity.

Infantile, that chaos in your hemispheres.
Infantile, but without the grace,
without the innocence of infancy.

Live now on the safe side of frontiers
and practise, practise anonymity.

At The Back Of My Mind

The little bit of brain that's literate –
the area in the left hemisphere
around the upper circle of the ear –
I use, or am used by, it to translate
electrochemical signals into words.
And since the brain's bridged by coaxial cords
I've words for wordless functions in the right
hemisphere, words for space and time and light
and music and...
                    And once again I hear
the grunting at the back of my mind where
my spine enters the curved base of my skull.
My brain stem, older than Neanderthal
man, needs words for semen, blood and shit.
I'm homo sapiens, and an animal.

In Two Minds

You think it's simply metaphorical,
that hypnagogic image of the fall
into the void that suddenly opens up
just as you hover on the edge of sleep?

It's a real fall into the real abyss
between your unconscious mind and consciousness.
Lose balance, and you fall into the cleft
between your brain's right hemisphere and its left.
At night your mind's off watch; one day your brain
might not let your mind back in again.

You say it's just a metaphorical cliff?
A metaphor like that can cost your life.
Not you? Not yet? Then may you never miss
your footing as you near the precipice.

3

Mind-reader 1
W G Penfield at the Montreal Neurological Institute 1934–60

The patients signed the forms, agreeing to take
enough only to block out pain and dull
the sound the saw made cutting through the skull.
The patients volunteered to stay awake
and talk to him as he probed the open brains.
He needed more than damaged tissue, malign
or mutant cells; he was trying to assign
functions to places, trying to map terrains
in living patients who were well and sane
enough to play this cerebral hide-and-seek,
conscious enough to speak to him. *(So speak,*
for God's sake. Speak! Before the cortocaine
wears off.) He moved the tiny stainless steel
electrodes once again. 'What do you feel?'

Mind-reader 2

Tumours, lesions, encephalopathies,
the merest aneurism in a vein
that leads blood through the networks of the brain –
sound-waves trace differences in density
between malignant tissue and benign.
A kiss of matter and antimatter scans
the brain for Alzheimer's or Parkinson's
disease, for signs of faults in the design.
In my case it was just an inner ear,
a labyrinthine anticlimax. But if
there's a next time I'll go back – half-deaf,
lopsided with tinnitus, grey with fear –
to the machine and trust it with my flawed
brain more readily than I'd trust a god.

(The scanning device in lines 4 and 5 is a magnetic resonance imaging
machine, MRI. The device in lines 6 to 8 is a positron emission tomography
machine, PET.)

Change Of Mind

So this is the sensation addicts kill
for and are killed, this simultaneous sense
of rapid time and time held in suspense,
of being host to an intelligence
that isn't mine but sets my conscious will
excitedly at ease and keeps vigil
with me and over me through the intense
tranquillity? There's little difference
between this state and the experience
of being on the poem's brink. I feel
the same hypnotic, psychotropic thrill
of parachuting through a focused trance
to this condition of deliverance
where poem and corpse on their white sheets lie still.

Boring Women

*After the visual illusion devised by the American psychologist E G
Boring, 1886–1963.*

The girl's right ear is the old woman's right eye
but the key to Boring's ambiguity
of youth and age lies in two curving black
lines converging as the focal point
of the picture. They form the taut right cheek
of the young woman learning how to flaunt
her pretty face in profile, her slim neck
by turning from –
                          She disappears. The gaunt
old woman gazes down the drooping beak
that is her nose; she's the inhabitant
of the same picture and the same –
                                               Her chic
companion re-appears, her elegant
head seen in the moment it turns away
from the death's head her pretty looks portray.

The Maze

Grey thorn trees shifting in a fine-blown dust –
that's my recurring image of the maze,
the state of mind in which the synapses
close down until transmission through the vast
network dries up. Simply because a phrase
is missing, or a single word, I'm cast
into the stupefaction that will cost
me hours or days. And so many new days
echo inside a dead day from the past
that the ashen tumulus outweighs
green time. I'm waiting for the trees to blaze
again with blossoming words, and the dust haze
to settle. I don't know how long this trust
in language, memory and mind can last.

The Mask

'Why poetry?' you asked, and triggered off
the sweaty, egocentric disarray
that claims me when I can't find the words' way
to the next line. I answered in my gruff
disdainful voice. I said, 'The brain's designed
to solve linguistic problems and to play
with language, meaning and reality.
A poem is the difference between mind
and brain.'
            Why did I give you that glib, brusque
reply? Because I couldn't make a bridge
to carry us beyond the wordless edge?
Because I couldn't change my ingrown mask?
That's what I'd tell you if you were to ask
again. But I know you won't repeat the risk.

Identity

An accident? Not quite, but I hadn't planned
on being like this. Identity redesigns
itself, its selves – my selves – along lines
I didn't choose and still don't understand
even now. There's fewer of them now,
fewer than the good, bright selves I've lost,
but there isn't one among this lot I'd trust
with another's life. Not one of them knows how
to be at peace, or simply to ignore
the others, let each other be. Instead,
each wants the others exiled, silenced, dead.
Who do these little bastards think they are?
I know. But how can they...? Or how can we...?
How can this be all that's left of me?

Sub-plot

I sit in silence listening to the chords
and rhythms of Bach and Bartok, Bird and birds.
I do most of my thinking without words.

What seem like dialogues inside my head
are sense impressions; nothing can be read
into them since nothing has been said.

Raking, spiking a lawn – that loosened state
of mind and body is lost when I translate
mowing, walking into the alphabet.

My brain decodes a million stimuli
unthinkingly. The pupils of my eyes
dilate, contract, involuntarily.

And there's the sub-text, or rather, the sub-plot:
I do most of my thinking without thought.

Childermas

Grunt. Back and – Grunt. And forward – Grunt. And back –
The boy rocks to and fro. He doesn't speak.

They were called wolf-children until we killed
the wolves; today we call these children wild.
To speak with love to children is to teach
children the mysteries of love and speech.
Silence and lovelessness sentence the child
to grunt in his bare room in his defiled
innocence. The silence will destroy
the child's capacity for mystery,
language and love. He grunts across the gulf
between the human animal and the wolf.

I write this poem as a childermas
for children cast into our wilderness.

Cosmos And Microcosmos
for Norman Thompson

The brain as microcosm? It seems a fair
analogy; there are as many cells
and synapses in the brain as there are stars
and constellations in the universe.

The cosmos as a brain? Then we would share
in an unlimited celestial
intelligence and prove the nebular
creation myth: all matter has its source
in the same gas and dust. But to compare
like this is fantasy. Comets don't trail
psychic metaphors through space; pulsars
aren't alpha rhythms from a friendly force.

We're on our own, watching the stars disperse
until earth's accident has run its course.

8

Canker

The flaw offended me.
I rubbed at the canker in the apple wood,
trying to finish the piece before the light failed.
But each new pass of the rasp
and each new cambium level exposed more decay.

I put away the tools
and then I waited, staring at the thing in the half-light.

Layers of sweat cooled to a single layer
as cold and heavy as a leaden shirt.
The sweat grew cooler still;
I felt a cold, dead skin inside my skin.

For hours the afterimage flickered on and off:
brown fungus spreading through the pale wood.
A phantom self inside me assumed a crouching stance,
hunched over the bench,
muscles tense in his shoulders, wrists and hands.

Because I'd stood too long at the task,
too long, and too rigidly intent on finishing the piece;
because I'd worked against time
and against the times and weathers in the changing widths of
                the grain –
because of these things
my body bent itself
and neurons fired their futile little flares
all evening around the canker in my mind.

Mistle Thrush

A mistle thrush was my way through the darkness
of Castle Hill Wood. The notes were streaks of light
in the January dawn. Through eight winters
the bird's song was a charm against madness.

Wrong. Eight years, and still the poem is wrong.

The six short phrases of the mistle thrush
are more than the thousands of pages I wrote
in that sick institute,
processing words, reprocessing processed words
until language was meaningless.

The poem is wrong because the bird and song
were formed so long before we lost our wings
and fell from the tree. Or fell, God's afterthought,
from the sky, or the tree in the sky.

So long, and the loud notes so absolute
that the music is incomprehensible.
And yet the spell of the bird's few syllables
is stronger than all those millions of words.

When I try to find words for the song
the bird stops singing.

I haven't heard the cycle of six phrases
sung as a single song. The mistle thrush sings
three of the phrases, and then five, and then two,
changing the order so that the sequence sounds new
each time I listen to it.

I listen, but I can't memorise the song.
The song has no beginning and no end,
and so the poem is wrong.

I hear the thrush singing through the sleet and snow
and flailing branches of a winter gale.
In spring's dawn chorus it's the soloist.
I hear it sing alone so late into the night
that I can barely see the silhouette –
the bird a black corn dolly
on the black haystack of the holly tree.

I wake and fall asleep to the song of the thrush.

Instalments

I have made ghosts of the living and the dead alike.

Is it too late, or can I still disguise
my lies as misremembered memories?

My brittle vanities needed an empty room,
a walled garden, a landscape without figures.
For company I had my peopled sleeplessness.

I lived mostly inside my fissured, whorled
brain; I thought it was a sufficient world.

I thought I was a bartering my soul for poetry.

Each night I met my friends inside my head;
it was a meeting of the living dead.

I forget. The neurons decay. I forget more and more.

My promises come back as crippled things,
poor homing pigeons trailing broken wings.

My fear is that I'll forget forgetfulness itself,
that the thing that's lost will be this sense of loss.

Late as it is, I still can't recognise
the difference between fact and fantasy.

Mysteries are fewer now: a mistle thrush tilting
the world on its axis at dawn in February,
the quickening conductivity of my brain
as I find these words in the clarity of this long twilight.

There's justice, then, in these recurrences,
the intermittent wordlessness, the wordless futility.
The disorders are instalments on my debts
of absence and vanity, and a fair price for poetry.

The guilty party pays the other's costs.
I make these severance payments to my ghosts.

Child's Play
for S G

Blue Shoes

The bluey bluenesses of blue:
pale shiny blue for toes and heels
with dark blue laces snaking through
and through and through the little holes.

The twoness of the things in twos:
hands and ears and eyes and nose,
the bluey twoness of her shoes,
two hands; two feet, two lots of toes.

The emptiness of empty shoes:
without her feet they look so light
she thinks her two blue shoes might choose
to run away from her one night.

But with loose laces in the eyes
and blue tongues loose in two shoes' faces,
they cannot run if no one ties
the loosened dark blue snaky laces.

Dot-to-Dot

Where's the princess? The tiny dots
keep joining up as sloping yachts
with slanting bowsprits, sails and spars
adrift on oddly-angled seas.

The princess? Dot-to-dot she plots
a course among the numbered spots
and charts a world of swirling stars,
snowflakes and flying Christmas trees.

Colouring, In The Car

Line after line the crayon tide
is coming in. She won't be sick
if her blue crayon strokes are quick
enough. Like this: from side to side,
flowing so fast that she can hide
herself in each blue wave. Traffic
is slowing down. The fumes are thick.
But she can make her crayon glide
faster across the page. The wide
white space is flooding with rhythmic
blue tidal waves, flick after flick
until it drowns the donkey guide
and children on the donkey ride.

Colouring is a better trick
than dot-to-dot arithmetic.
She won't be sick. She won't be sick.

Dreaming

She lies awake because she fears
that when she falls asleep she'll fall
into the otherworld of dreams
so far from home that no one hears
her cry for help; her voice so small
and far that no one hears her screams;
so far she might not re-appear
in time to hear her mother call
her name next morning. Name... Her name...
She could be lost for years and years.
She might not get back home at all.
Or wake to find she's not the same
child who fell asleep. Her name...
Her name is sounding in her ears.

Waking Time

But how can it be time to rise?
How can it be morning time
when all she did was blink her eyes
a moment ago? Or time to climb
from bed when it's still yesterday?
If this is morning, where did last
night go? Why did it go away?
How can time disappear so fast?

She hadn't seen the darkness creep
across her room, across the sky;
she had fallen so fast asleep
that time and darkness passed her by.

Woman In The Hospice

On a Greek island thirty years ago
he said, 'The secret's to anaesthetise
our short-term memories and feel time slow
to a standstill. This way to paradise.'

After the first two days I forgot the date.
The radio and television were Greek.
And then two days, or three days, after that
I didn't even know the day of the week.

I felt uneasy; if we lost all track
of time we wouldn't know the day our lease
expired. He said, 'Darling, we're not going back.
We're going to live forever here in Greece.'

Gradually, I learned how to relax
with him: the sea, the wine, the summer heat
and lovemaking that was both love and sex.
He said, 'This island is a timeless state.

'I'm drowning in the azure of your eyes.
They're bluer than the silk dome of the sky
or the Aegean's blue translucencies.'
He called me Lady Lapis Lazuli.

You think it's stupid of me to recall
these things now? Stupid to put my trust
in memories after an interval
of thirty years? Perhaps. But I have lost

All track of time again since I came here.
Is it because the drugs induce a sense
of freedom, killing not just pain but the fear
of death by cancelling the future tense?

It must be drugs. It's certainly not wine,
warm sea, blue sky, sex in the lemon grove.
And yet I feel more peace than the morphine
alone can give. There's love, something like love

In this place, in this sweet state between sleep
and waking, this condition between time
and stillness, timelessness, that's mine to keep.
Love and drugs admit me to the dream.

The Price Of Tea

He looked at me, said nothing, and looked away
to ask someone behind me as I passed by.

His training shoes and heavy overcoat,
the way he whispered the question to himself
before he said it aloud, and when he spoke:
'Scuse me. Spare the price of a cup of tea?'
the gurgle of emphysema in his throat –
I couldn't doubt his authenticity.

They used to stop me in the street. Not now.
They can see my double chin, the middle-age paunch
that even my new tweed jackets can't conceal.
They can read between the lines the middle-class
hatreds and anxieties in my face.
My face, my hurried walk, my date for lunch…
The beggar looked at me, and let me pass.

He caught my eye and saw in that quick glance
my sunken, cloudy-grey indifference.

The way he turned side-on, the way he stooped
and had to look up from the pavement's edge,
his face in semi-profile… About my age?
His right arm at half-stretch, the hand half-cupped…
About my age. And he'd be about my height
inside that overcoat if he stood straight.

I checked my small change: Fifty pence? A pound?
After lunch, perhaps. If he's still around.

Musical Encounters:
A Radio 3 Fantasy

Two seconds? Three? Not more than five
and yet the silence sounds longer,
the silence between your last syllable
and the moment the disc begins to play.

And when the music ends
there's another silence, different,
before you begin to speak to me again.

Your voice is magnified by silences.
I turn the volume down
and still your words sound amplified, enlarged,
as if your studio voice is slightly slower...
slower... and lower by half an octave
than the voices of your other selves.

But I can hardly hear you breathe.
Do you turn your head away from the microphone
or is one quick intake, that barely audible ah,
enough for each introduction?

I hear the separate strands of sound in your voice;
each word you speak is a chord.

You speak in sentences, faultlessly, from your own script.
And each brief commentary is a prelude,
one of the suite of preludes only you can play.
You play a new suite once, and then abandon it.

Each piece of music you introduce
ends as an introduction
to the incidental music of your voice.

Your disembodied voice grows visible.
Your voice assumes a palpable shapeliness.

Do you speak to him like this on the telephone?
Do you speak like this to him in the night?
Has he felt the sound of your breath on his neck?
Has he seen you wordless, gasping for breath?

And has he told you? Has he told you
he hardly dares to listen to your programme,
Musical Encounters, because he knows that I –
and I, and I, and I, – am listening too?

Because your studio voice
reading your scripts to me like love letters
is the voice of someone he can never know.

The Vanishing Parakeet

Say a word aloud. Say *parakeet*
aloud. Say *parakeet* aloud again:
parakeet. And once more: *parakeet.*
The parakeet begins to moult; the bird
begins to disappear into the sound.

Mouth *parakeet* as if aloud, with lips,
tongue, throat, teeth – *pa, ra, kee, eet,* – *parakeet.*
The twittering screech is barely audible.
Your mouth is silencing the parakeet.
The sound is disappearing in the word.

Parakeet. Another *parakeet*
till *parakeet* is no more than a set
of tiny muscles flexing, facial nerves
twitching, twitching. And a synapse pulsing
automatically in your brain.

Parakeet. The word's now meaningless,
silent – *parakeet* – invisible:
a perfect hiding place for parakeet.

19

Neurological Rounds

Mr William Sloane. Age 44

'Lesions in Broca's area. He had a fall.'

Where did she say? It was in Ashton Street.
I was doing the even numbers in Ashton Street.

'Thank you, Sister. Good morning, Mr Sloane.
What can you tell me about yourself this morning?'

'Pain... tuh... pain...'
Long ago, but I've seen these two before.
'Pain... tuh... pain... tuh... ray...'
I was never much of a talker but this is mince.
How did I get so far from Ashton Street?

'Pain? An X-ray to locate the pain?'

'I think Mr Sloane's telling us
he's a painter, a painter and decorator.'

'Yes. Aphasia. Certainly. Yes. And Broca's? Yes.
Now I should like to hear some more of him.'

'Do you know why you're here, Mr Sloane?
Can you tell Mr Makjian why you're here?'

Does she mean why I'm *here? This* hospital?
Meaning mental. But it's just the words.
I thought the Vicky or the Western G,
being the nearest to Ashton Street.
Thank God it's just a phase. 'Loss... loss... wors...'
Surely to God they know it's just the words.
Inside my head the words sound fine. The words.
The words. I just can't get them out.
Can't get them from my brain to my mouth.
'Loss... fuh... loss... fuh... wors...'
But not mad. 'Not... not... mmm...'
Shut it, Sloaney. Find another word.

She asked you if you knew why you were here.
'Fall... fall... fall...'

'Splendid, Mr Sloane. You had a fall.
What can you remember about your fall?'

'Effing... evering... effering...'
The sun, the sun on my back, and the smell
of primer covering up the smell of scorch
where I'd burned off and sanded the day before.
'Pain... ti... pain... ti...'
Ing, for God's sake, Sloaney. Ing as in ing.
'Pain... ti... painti... winnow... fame...'
The brush going to and fro, the easy flow
of primer whitening the window frame.
And the funny feeling, the lovely feeling you feel
when you stand at the top of the ladder, the sun on your back,
and watch yourself watching the brush going to and fro.
An upstairs window. The even side of Ashton Street.
'Jam... uh... jam... winnow... frame...'
A heave at the frame. Another heave –
'Fall... een... tide... uh... slide... fall...
evenside... uh... Ashn... Ashton Street...'

'You were painting window frames on the even side,
the even number side, of Ashton Street
and then you fell. Splendid, Mr Sloane.
Splendid. You remember everything.'

Everything? One second? Two seconds?
Falling a long, long time.
This morning? Falling. Yesterday? Last week?

'Sister, how soon can therapy begin?
Tomorrow. Yes. Tomorrow, Mr Sloane.'

But there's therapy and therapy.
There's physio and then there's –
Don't say it, Sloaney. You couldn't, anyway.
Try physio. 'Physi... phys... uh... physi... o...'

'It may persist, the fizzing in your head.
The lesions in Broca's area, that is…'
The polysynaptic reflex arc. 'The left
hemisphere…' The inferior frontal lobe.
'Your left ear, Mr Sloane, not the ear itself
but… How would you say it, Sister?'

'Just above your left ear, Mr Sloane.
Imagine a little area inside your head
just above and in front of your left ear.
Your fall has damaged the little bit of your brain
that helps you to speak, and read and write.'

Signwriting as well?
I was never much of a talker, a reader or writer.
But the signwriting:
black Roman capitals of Andrew Strang,
Rods & Guns since 1899;
the Gothic gold of Antique Maps and Prints;
the slim italics of computafile.

'Mr Makjian thinks speech therapy might help
in your case, but there's no guarantee.
We'll see what Mrs Scott says tomorrow morning.'

Speech therapy. Thank God for that.
Did she say that before? Speech therapy?
The same bit of time seems to happen a second time.
And then there's gaps when there's nothing, no time at all.
And times when different bits of time –
breakfast, then breakfast again, and breakfast again,
birds singing in the middle of the night –
when different bits of time get all mixed up.

'Mr Makjian can't make promises
because we can't repair your synapses,
the little junction boxes in your brain,
transformers and transducers.
But you'll still be able to do everything else.'

I couldn't do as much as that before.

'Your job, for instance. You'll still be able to paint.
And gardening. Are you a gardener?
No? There's lots of other things, Mr Sloane:
walking, swimming, or even a little jogging;
driving, travelling, sightseeing;
darts or drafts or dominoes or bowls.'

Oh aye? I wish I'd fell off years ago.

'Radio, television, photography.
You could even try your hand at something new:
angling, cooking, music, home-made wine.
Yes. Why don't you try your hand at something new?
After all, you're a different person now.'

Different? I thought she said it's just a phase.
'Not... a... phase... a... phase...?'

'Yes, Mr Sloane. Aphasia. Loss of speech.
Some reading and writing also will be lost,
but all the properties of your right hemisphere,
that is, your visuospatial skills... I mean –
Sketching. You will do sketching, Mr Sloane,
and all the splendid things that Sister said.'

Sketching. Aye. I like the sound of that.
Sketching and therapy, speech therapy.
And this feeling, this daft feeling again,
top-of-the-ladder feeling, the sun on my back
now that I know what's happening. 'Ha... hap...
happe...' Try glad, for God's sake, Sloaney.
'Glad... glad... tuh... hap... hap... happe...'

'You are glad and happy, Mr Sloane?
Splendid. Tomorrow therapy begins.
I shall return on Friday, Mr Sloane.
We shall have another splendid chat.'

* * *

'He speaks as if he were inventing speech.[9]
The network damaged, without synapses
for grammar or syntax, is a new network,
each word uttered as if for the first time
and with the artlessness of first attempts.
The simplest form, the simplest sound of the word:
nouns, but no plural nouns;
verbs without a past or future tense;
not "I have fallen" or "I shall fall"
but the stammering, unconditional simplicity –
"Fall. Fall. Fall."
No. No. I speak like a barbarian.
Mr Sloane, he has sensation still
and memory enough to make a world.'

'Yes. A solitary man like Mr Sloane
may need few words, or none, to accept himself,
while Mr Crosier there…
He's certainly making up for lost time
now that he knows he's still alive.
He was so sad when he finally opened his eyes.
"I was quite safe," he said. "You needn't have
brought me back again. I was quite safe."'

Mr R S Crosier. Age 73

'Good morning, Mr Crosier. How are you?
What can you tell Mr Makjian this morning?'

'Good morning to you. I am morning.
Sir, I say you are no starry paladin
but a reprician – reprician – reprician –
But I diverse, and I apologise.
I say you are patrublican –
partrub – patrib – patrublican.
In otherliness you are repatrian.'

'You are very generous, Mr Crosier.
Others deserve your kindness more than I.
Sister Murray here, and Mrs Scott.'

'I understand. Firenze – Firenze luscinia
and all immately larchicals, without whom
I have no sleeping now or waking then.
But you, young sir – Although I am old
and speak my age I am as morning
in the good morning of repatrians.'

'Splendid, Mr Crosier. Your speech improves.
And you co-operate with Mrs Scott?'

'In principling but not in genesis –
suffix – genesis – suffix – No, sir. No.
You are the refutable suffix of your suffix.
The confutable of your suffix.
In otherliness the herisable nymbus.
Herisable suffix of your nymbus.'

'You mean my name? My nationality?'

'No, no, young sir. I do apologise.
The principling of statelessness –
I hear my voice diverse again.'

'Your voice is clear, Mr Crosier.'

'My voice is clear, sir, and I say to you,
you are of the eagle stockists and patrublicans.
Repatrian as I once wished to be;
as you are now, sir, and shall be.
I must not halt your pilgrimage
but I say these things while I am morning,
while there are chalices – chalices –
while there are galaxies inside your head.
Not Avalon, sir. Never Avalon.
In my head once, and now in yours, young sir.'

'I am most grateful, Mr Crosier.
Republic or kingdom? It is enough to know
we recognise the same infinity.
On Friday you will tell me more
for I have much to learn.'

'Just rest now, Mr Crosier. I'll come for you
at half-past ten and take you to Mrs Scott.'

* * *

'One of the other sisters on the course
said it was just like someone speaking in tongues.
You weren't meant to hear her but you did
and for a moment you looked ill with rage.
"Divinity?" you said. "Divinely inspired?
Possessed by a holy spirit? A holy ghost?"
And then your anger turned to sarcasm:
"Or do you think religious ecstasy
is caused by lesions in the frontal lobe?"
Tap-tap-tapping with your fingertips
behind your left ear; rapid little thuds.
"A holy ghost with Wernicke's aphasia?"
Somebody laughed. You wavered, and then smiled
and went on lecturing. At the end you said
the intervention of the holy ghost
had made that lecture memorable.'

'I meant my anger. I apologise.'

'No. I remember some of the arithmetic:
ten billion neurons and ten billion more
synapses – Mr Crosier's galaxies? –
and half a million words and variants,
and personal accent and vocabulary –
you clicked a slide: *Lexicon, Idiolect* –
that make each person's speech unique.
You got us thoroughly confused and then you said
the figures proved we must not hope to find
meaning in the Wernicke aphasic's speech.
"You may hear a greater frequency
of abstract nouns," you said, "or passive verbs,
but what you hear is the patient's patholect,
sound and meaning irreparably split
in a non-language we cannot translate
because we have no code." Another slide:
Phonology, Semantics, Patholect.

26

We were hopelessly confused. "Listen," you said,
"listen to tone and quality of voice,
the tempo, volume, rhythm and the pitch.
You must tell your patients this," you said;
"your patients and your nurses and yourselves:
Aphasia means that language has been lost
and the lost words may never again be found,
but the patients still have power to think and feel.
Aphasia means a small part of the brain
is lost; the patients have not lost their minds."'

'I said these things. Yes. You remember well.
And you remember there was something more?'

'Yes. "When the patients take our word for it..."'

Mr Charles Guthrie. Age 56

'Concussion, is it? There's no smell of drink.
We found him wandering on the motorway.
No car. No keys. Looks like a hit and run,
but where did he think he was going, poor old sod,
at three in the morning on the motorway?'

* * *

'"And when the patients take our word for it?"
Then we discharge them, Sister. We turn them out.
Mr Guthrie? I think that he begins
to understand the nature of his loss,
the arc of fibres linking sound and sense.
Sever the arcuate fasciculus
and speech is simply atmospheric noise,
an interference with whatever truce
he may have begun to make for himself.
He may adopt deafness as a stratagem
against bewilderment and the hiss
and cackle of static that pours from people's mouths.
He may become convinced that he is deaf

or word-deaf because the spoken word
no longer makes sense to him, or even non-sense.
But while he knows he is not going deaf
or mad, and has not lost his memory,
and now that we know his name, his next of kin
and his address, Sister, we turn him out.'

* * *

The doctor's speaking and I hear the words
but only for the time it takes to say
whatever it is he's saying to me now
and then there isn't time his words are gone.

Not deaf. I hear him clearly but he speaks
too fast he leaves no space between one word
and the next too fast between each breath
a burst of words in one rushed single word.

I choose my words I choose before I speak
I speak them carefully but I can't hear
if the words I'm saying are the words I chose.
Words disappear as soon as they are said.

2 Memory Traces

Thomas Hardy At
Stinsford Churchyard, 1927

for Andrew Johnstone, Douglas Kilpatrick and George Macadam

Centuries

The churchyard is so full of death
that what was once a level ground,
an acre reclaimed from the heath,
is now a place where two great mounds
are growing from the earth beneath.

They rise like two green hills, each crowned
with stones that look like monoliths
on tumuli. The hills confound:
it is as if the sunken paths
do not lead to the church but round

And down into the green hills' myths
of skulls and crucifixes, down
and down to the bare bones of faith
where centuries of death are bound
together in the living earth.

What The Gravedigger Said

'Ashes to ashes…' Padre opens his fist:
the ball of loam bursts with the little gasp
and scatters across the oak lid like the rasp
of scurrying rats. Padre says 'Dust to dust…'

The sound of it, the sight of where we all
must come, can twist a mourner's face from grief
to terror. An afterlife? Aye, after life
the body lies beneath a ton of soil.

You ask again – 'The body after death?' –
As if you already knew and wanted now
to match my lore against yours and see how
far I'll trust a stranger with my truth.

The knowledge seems unnatural, unclean
to those who are so fearful of the facts
that follow death, yet they are gentle acts
of cleansing. Let me tell you what I've seen.

As soon as the heart stops beating it begins
to rot from the inside. Maggots and worms?
They can't do beeswaxed oak or pine much harm;
coffins decay like corpses, from within.

And while flesh is unfastening from bone,
the brain and eyes are seeping from the skull,
sinews and skin are rendered down until
the little deaths that follow death are done.

I've seen the little deaths, and I see why
the knowledge of them sets a man apart
from other men. Some call it a black art
to know the ways of bodies when they die.

Black or white, an art or craft or trade –
Call it what they will, they all come here
for that last gentle cleansing. Year by year
I care less for the living than the dead.

31

What The Gardener Said

A day of darkness and light
and all the shadows between morning and night.
A day of skies
and then the fashioning of boundaries
of oceans, lands and lakes.
And in the same day, before woman, man or snake,
there was the making of trees.

Until our forfeiture
of the dream, trees were the earth's first creatures,
the wisest and loveliest.
We adorned the great oaks and the yews, dressed
them with skulls
and slaked their thirst with the blood of the white bull.
We were children of the forest.

We forfeited the dream
for our awakening to iron, fire and time.
A sleepless sky god
taught us new laws of life and death, of good
and evil, promised us love
if we would take fire and iron into the groves.
We felled and burned the woods.

What we could not kill
we called superstition, then folly, then child's play, until
Maypole and May Queen,
Mummers and Morris Men, Green Man and Jack-in-the-
Green
danced between the new faith
and the stumps and smouldering ashes of the heath,
scrubland, forest and fen.

The trees, sir, in this arch
that stands between the graveyard and the church;
these yews are seeded from
parent plants older by far than Christendom.
And all our christenings
will not wash away the knowledge of these things.

Sir, the skies are darkening.
You say that you have reached the end of your search?
I wish you safely home.

What The Stonemason Said

Frost and wind and time and rain
on granite, sandstone, slate or marble
write their dead language and garble
God's words and mine.

Rain and frost and wind and time
on marble, granite, sandstone or slate
wipe away the age, the date
and the dead name.

Time and rain and frost and wind
on slate, marble, granite or sandstone
gnaw until their work is done
and my words end.

Wind and time and rain and frost
on sandstone, slate, marble or granite
pronounce the only lasting rite
in words of moss.

Druid Cosmology

God lives inside my head
because I live in his;
for God is earth, moon, sun
and everything that is beneath the sun.

Living inside his head,
I know his laws are made
for earth and moon and sun, and not for men.

With one chill breath he fells
a hill of pines as if the trees were children.

Soil grows hard as rock
and grass is brittle as glass in our horses' mouths.

Yet with another breath
ice thaws and the hazel buds begin to uncurl.

We raise Godstones for fear
of his long tongues of fire,
for fear of his roaring among the mountain tops.

We raise Godstones
to mark the lightest and the darkest of his days.

At night his inward eyes,
his many eyes look down,
watching us, watching our dreams, and glittering, glittering.

A Winter Fugue

for Lesley Brocklebank

Geese are flying from one feeding ground
to another, an easy inland flight
and yet the birds are calling ceaselessly
to keep their pace and height, to keep their tight
formation like a skiff of visible sound
trailing its audible wake across the sky.

Nearer, I can hear the separate cries,
alternating notes of differing pitch
that rise and fall in fluctuating streams
of rapid overlapping rhythm. As each
goose calls in time so the geese improvise
their variations on original themes.

Goose music is a roll-call against squalls
of hail, a counterpoint against the long
darkness. Goose music is itself a force
of nature and the geese are syllables
in a fugue that's two-in-one, both song
and winter flight across the Stirling carse.

Light Measures

Night Snow

Big, wet flakes were falling fast and straight
out of the void into the ring of light.

I looked so long at the fast-falling snow,
letting my field of vision come and go –
from the white surface of the window ledge
to the black shape and shadow of the hedge,
and upwards from the disappearing grass
to the surrounding dome of nothingness –
I looked so long at it I could not tell
the snow that was illusory from the real.

Snowflakes fall like snowflakes in a dream
of time; like particles of time they stream
in a continuum of here and now
yet even as I watched, the fallen snow
was melting into the past. Snowflakes fall
like visible silences that overspill
from gardens into streets until the white
soundlessness of snowfall fills the night.

Big, wet flakes of snow were falling thick
and fast and randomly, yet by some trick
of repetition and multiplicity
the randomness grew rhythmic, orderly.
And by some trick of movement through the night
sky, thick flakes fell slower till their flight
became this hovering, half-lit from below,
this ceaseless, stationary, fast-falling, slow
delirium of silence, time and snow.

Sun, Stone, Water

Mist thinned on the last half-mile.
The January air was laced with particles of light.

The waterfall erupting
from the frozen hill
was a blinding iridescence of tears and ice.

We were above the layers of mist.
Sun shone on the waterfall,
scattering cataracts of shattered light across the morning.

On the way back
we watched the river gather faltering streams,
leading them down
through rock gorges
to the black trees dripping liquid mist,
to the meadows
and the rooftops of the little town
fashioned from sun and stone and running water.

Sky, Sea, Earth

In the long afterglow
the sky glistens like a beach between tides.
The wavering repetition
of overlapping bars of sea-water and shore-sand,
ribs of silver and blue stippled with strips of gold –
the wavering repetition
ripples all the way down to the horizon.

Light ebbs into the red vortex.

Gloaming seeps across fields
like a tide rising, purpling,
the purple rising and deepening,
levelling all the undulations of light and shade,
evening its own unevenness
until a moment of equinoctial clarity
simplifies the darkening earth and sky.

Lovers' River

The little river runs
beneath green canopies
of hazel, alder, birch.

The little river runs
like lovers murmuring,
whispering, murmuring
in a green light that is
the light of dawn and dusk.

All through the murmuring night
the lovers' river runs.

Hedgerows

The wild rose and the rowan tree,
bramble, hawthorn, elderberry –
the high hedgerows and garlanded
with pink and purple, black and red
beads from a broken rosary.

Dry-stone Wall In Westmorland

The hill was roughly ploughed for Sitka spruce.
Now the land is swallowing the first course of the wall
and loosening all the others.
Fallen stones are being sucked down into the earth again.

On marginal lands hill farmers harvested stones,
gathered them and graded them as a crop
on hills with soil too shallow to hold a fence post;
too shallow to hold anything
but bracken, heather, thin grass, sheep and men.

In the high, stony shires –
Inverness, Argyll and here in Westmorland –
hundreds of miles of dry-stone walls are falling.
The boundaries they once marked have been redrawn
on computer software, the divisions overgrown
by the closed ranks of Alaskan Sitkas.

Far from their arctic origins
the trees are rampant in these temperate latitudes.
They smother the occasional alder, hazel or birch.
They dwarf the small farmhouses
on the hills above Lochaber, Inveraray and Appleby.

Mossed, lichened, this man-made wall in Westmorland
looks more natural than the Sitkas dismantling it.

Canada –
Awakening The Trees

From the Notebook of Patrick Napier

The Company Of Trees

No, I do not believe that trees have souls
But I enjoy the company of trees.
Then do I practise solitude? Perhaps
I am as much a creature of the forest
As of the town. No, I do not abhor
The heathenism of the Indians
Or the Métis.
                              I write this in my book
But dare not play denials with the man
Lest I disturb my hibernating beast
And find it more ungovernable than the God
Whom Monsieur Taillandier cannot forgive.

Plague Carrier

I came ashore like a refugee from plague
And found the fever was already here,
Urgent, unslakeable and driving me
From place to place until there was no doubt:
The malady was in my mind; it fouled
My thoughts like poisoned water in a well.

Tic and tremor in my eye and hand.
Anger and sadness. Anger and sadness. Waves
Of sundering anger. And my thumping heart
Absurdly alternating Charge! Retreat!
Troughs of extravagant, unfounded grief.
My dry throat palpitating like a frog's.

In The Compass Of A Tree

I leaned against a maple tree. I closed
My eyes and breathed as if I were asleep
In the cool scented compass of the tree.
I sensed the pale leaves moving in the wind
And whispering distantly like audible stars.
I felt the intricate simplicity
Of purpose in the tree. I opened my eyes
Again but I was still asleep. I saw
Beauty in the irregularities
Of trunks and branches, buds and leaves and crowns
Of maple trees and walnut, elm and oak,
Snowy mespil, persimmon and lime.
I saw the trees' benign indifference
And knew it was companionship enough.

And since the trees have neither minds nor souls
Their beauty cannot be a state of grace.
They are a form of unregenerate life
Lower than creaturehood and yet above
All other things. How strange that trees should be
Not supernatural but natural.

Frost

Trees are seldom wholly silent or still.
In the great frost, the coldest I have known
Since my first voyage on the *Challenger,*
When nothing moved and the whole land was dumb
With snow, I heard faint creakings in the trunks
Of sugar maples as the frozen sap
Expanded. I remembered the small sounds
The *Challenger* made at anchor in the night.

'Listen. Do you hear him?' the Indian said.
'The spirit of the tree cries out with cold.'

41

Thaw

The spirits weep with joy, the Indian
Might say of ash trees on a day like this
When April sunlight is just warm enough
To thaw the hoarfrost on the leafless twigs.

I am content to feel the melting frost
Drip on my head and on my upturned face
And in my eyes as if the tears were mine.

The Forgetting Of The Songs – What the Indian Said

To forget the forgetting of the songs.
River. The song of the river. Forget.
The song of every tribe of animal and bird and tree.
The song of the stars. Forget. The stars. Forget. The moon.

We sang the songs. Sang. Sang the songs.
Songs sang in our mouths
And we knew the path that would lead us through the forest.
Singing. And across the icefield. Singing.

Lost. Forget the songs. Whisky. Lost.
Whisky to forget the forgetting of the songs.
Whisky. Swallow forgetting. Swallowing.
And fall again into the whirlpool.

The whirlpool is Jouskeha singing.
Singing the swallowing song that drags me down
And down with all the animals and birds and trees.
Down. And falling stars. Down. And the moon. Falling.

Song? Song of songs?
Sun-song before the whirlpool?
Whisky and sun-song before the forgetting?
And then the whirlpool. Swallowing.

42

Jouskeha's swallowing song, the whirlpool.
Sun-song? Forget. Forget.
Jouskeha's song of unmaking. Forget. Forget.
Swallowing all for the forgetting of the songs.

Curing The Indians

The willow man, the keeper of the songs,
The healer, the astronomer and the priest –
The Indian told me how his kinsmen died:
One taken by wolves and one crushed by a tree;
'Eaten by tree' was what the Indian said.
Another entered the river and was drowned,
And one was seized by a thunderbolt, he said.

The Indian is deranged by alcohol.
He jabbers in wild English, Iroquois
And a third tongue no one has heard before.
His every utterance is fantasy
Or lamentation, like those Highlanders
Whom we left weeping on the quay at Leith,
Too drunk and broken to board the *Belvedere.*

And then the Indian spoke as if one man
Had died these deaths, died and returned to life
Year after year until the final death.
'C'était une résurrection toute paienne,
Une participation mystique,'
Taillandier said. 'Maintenant ils sont guéris.'
He smothered his grunt of laughter in a cough.

'The river,' the Indian cried. 'The river is red.'
On other days he says the river runs black.
Cured, by God? The Indians are cured?
He says he can no longer find his way
Alone through the forest. 'The trees,' he cries,
'The trees are changing places in the night
And when I waken everything is lost.'

Drawing A Tree

I dip my pen and try to draw a tree:
A round white cloud is anchored to the earth.
I try again: ten fingers, crooked, black,
Of someone buried alive. And once again:
A lacework of black veins and arteries
Reaches from heaven to earth. I dip and draw
A weeping birch: the Indian's long black hair
Makes him an animal without a face.

An Oak Millennium

Now that I have some French I am unsure
Of Père Taillandier. What I had thought
Was righteousness now sounds like epigram.
He told me that the oak he felled last week
Had stood five centuries. Could this be so?

'Napier, vous êtes un homme sans chaines.
Deux chênes – et voila votre millénaire,
Le paradis terrestre dans les arbres.'
A smile. He ridicules me, or himself?
A grunt of laughter smothered in a cough.

I asked him why his men had felled the tree.

'Le paradis – c'est un grand encombrement
A l'église.' Like curing Indians,
I thought. Again the smile, the little cough.
Not cynicism but complicity?
With Indians and Métis and with me.
And with the forest? 'Pas un encombrement,'
I mumbled in reply, 'mais l'église même?'

Five hundred years felled in a single day.

'Peut-être, Napier,' Taillandier said.
He neither smiled nor coughed as he turned away
And walked back to his little wooden church.

Awakening The Trees

The Indian asked if I would go with him.
The wind was fierce. There was a racing moon
And yet the air surprised me with its warmth.

In each black oak a set of organ pipes –
Echo and solo, swell and great and choir –
Played bass to treble simultaneously.

And through the branches of the hazel trees
The fluctuating melody and drone
of bagpipes playing pibrochs in the night.

'Jouskeha is awakening the trees,'
The Indian sang, and he began to dance
A shuffling little dance in the April night.

I shuffled too. I heard his moaning song
Among the moaning oaks. 'The trees,' I cried.
'Jouskeha is awakening the trees.'

Patrick Napier was commissioned in the Royal Navy from 1873, and served as a sub-lieutenant on *HMS Challenger* on its voyage to the Antarctic in 1874. When illness forced him to retire from the navy in 1881 or 1882, Napier spent some years travelling in Canada before returning to Scotland in 1889.

Trumpet Variations
After John Wallace in Dunblane Cathedral
for Gordon Lang

Vaulted space delays the time signature:
you breathe immediacy
into your repertoire
and yet the notes hang longer in the air.
As we listen to you play
we drop our temporal disguise and share
your reading of immortality.

Part of the brain's designed to conjure sounds
and if by chance –
the obsessive trance that so confounds
and disconcerts us that we call it deviance –
if that bit of the brain gains dominance
it orchestrates all else around
the sway of the neurons' dance.

From the open window of the studio
and from the academy,
from beyond the gulag's walls of snow
and from the ghetto
they rise from the page, from the scored memory,
the little notes. In their own time they go
wriggling, fluttering towards eternity.

And the brain's programmed to convert
each sound into the symbol
that is its counterpart.
But what the symbol and the sound both chart –
systole, diastole –
is the speechless phonetic language of the heart
and the soul.

You play at tempos faster than the speed
of thought or speech,
and slower than dreams. There's no rational need
for any of this, but for a time we're freed
from time as we reach
across octaves, centuries, following the lead
of your perfect pitch.

Ariel With A Saxophone, Prospero With A Piano – Paul Desmond and Dave Brubeck

Brubeck pretends he's tuning the piano.

We grow breathless waiting for Desmond to breathe again
as he follows himself following
a mind designed for flight
through these inexhaustible shy certainties.

Brubeck is scattering scales with his right hand
and catching some of them with his left.

Notes chosen at the unrepeatable moment of utterance
have instantaneous composure,
the secret wild familiarity
of Desmond echoing the music of the spheres.

Brubeck finds the wrong note he's been looking for.
He strikes it again and again until it sounds right.

Desmond plays his new arrangements of the mysteries
of time and sound and silence,
and plays his own antiphony
through the golden numbers of his long fugue.

Brubeck's right hand is playing a one-two-three waltz.
His left is tapping a source of oracular chords.

Desmond closes his eyes.
Boundaries are flying around him
like garlands shedding petals in the breeze.

Edward Thomas
Embarkation Leave, December 1916
for William Paxton and John Thompson

Cathedral

The smell of many candles snuffed,
darkness and then the sickly waft
of molten wax with that charred tang
of desolation on my tongue.
I think of bodies burned to ash,
of bodies gutted and the flesh
embalmed. I think with every breath
I take I taste the spores of death.

I knew I should find nothing here
but did not guess at such despair
as this. In the cathedral gloom
the smooth grey sandstone pillars gleam
like great beech trees in the half-light
between heaven and earth, bearing the weight
of fear and faith.
              I make my way
beneath the beech wood's canopy.

The Path Through The Wood

Mosses are spreading and small grasses growing,
hollows are filling up with fallen leaves
and only the worn stony places are showing
the narrow course the path makes through the trees.

Whoever trod this path has gone away.

I walk alone, without maps, lingering
for larks' song, running water, otters' spoor
yet seeking more than these, hungering
for demons of the glade, the gorge, the tor.

I would be pilgrim but I cannot pray.

Demons? I seek no ordinary haunting
by ghosts or gods but creatures natural
and earthly as I am. I am hunting
an order of creation before the fall.

With neither maps nor faith I go astray.

The wood is growing dark. I walk on, casting
no shadow on my wayside shrines of white
birch beside the half-seen path, trusting
the thrush that's singing in the fading light.

Then have I chanced on the lost trysting-way?

Even as I make my last thanksgiving
at the wood's edge, I know I will not find
stillness enough; more and more I am living
in the sundered country of my mind.

I have walked the goodness out of another day.

Rain

An hour ago when I resumed my walk
this upstart river on its bed of chalk
and loose flints was a dusty Shropshire lane.

Skies darker than the earth have come so near
that steeples, towers, treetops disappear.
I lose my landmarks in this new terrain.

Thunder is quarrying the cliffs of heaven;
there is no nesting place for dove or raven.
I think the world will never be dry again.

The only source of light is the flickering tongues
of the celestial snakes, the only songs
their gasp of hunger and their roar of pain.

My feet are churning soil to mud and slime.
I walk in darkness on the edge of time.
The end should come in heavy and lasting rain.

In The Middle Of The Wood

This stillness in the middle of the wood
is just as true and natural a force
as the west wind that flows around the elms
at the wood's edge. No bird has hardihood
enough to fly or forage in that fierce
power, and yet it cannot overwhelm
the still centre. Instead, the wind's subdued
by stillness, baffled by it, turned off course
to circumnavigate this little realm
that is unruffled in the buffeting flood
of rushing air and is itself a source
of the simplicity I need, the calm
at the storm's centre, stillness neither good
nor evil in the middle of the wood.

Walking Home

It wasn't the storm clouds mustering
in a night sky with neither moon nor stars,
　　　or the December wind blustering
across the sodden fields and through the sparse
　　　hedgerows. It was a festering
sore of my own making – Outcast. Exile. –
the long estrangement of that final mile.

　　　I walked on in my covering
of sleet and rain. The comfortable sweat
　　　had chilled, and I was shivering
with cold and the cold fear of how complete
　　　had been the last mile's severing
of task from purpose, the journey from the goal.
I felt the frost spread outwards from my soul.

　　　I was a child again, mumbling
'The Angel Gabriel' through my chittering teeth
　　　but the sleety wind was fumbling
at my numb mouth while brain and gasping breath
　　　and feet were stumbling
the frozen measures of my self-deceit,
each to a different, stiffening, slow beat.

　　　The Loughton fields were glittering
with ice when I reached home. The kitchen fire
　　　was still alight and sputtering
with little tongues of singing flame, a choir
　　　of glowing coals unfettering
the spirits of a forest that had drowned
a million years ago. Dear ghosts, I found
　　　such warmth in your chattering
and hope of homecoming however far
I have to travel in a world at war.

Memory Traces

Thresholds

To come in from the garden's summer light
and think you've crossed the threshold between sight
and nothingness because each room is blind
with smoke... To wake up in the night to find
your pillow soaked with blood, your mouth, your nose
sticky with blood and yet to wonder whose
the blood can be... To listen to the pitch
of your voice rising, breaking in a screech
of puny rage... is to know these intense
wild bits and pieces of experience –
so vivid that they seem hallucinatory –
filed instantly as long-term memory.
And know year after year your mind will stage
black comedies of smoke and blood and rage.

The Code

They're no more ours than the flock of waxwings
that broke their flight just long enough to tear
the last few berries from the whitebeam trees
across the street. And when the trees were bare
the birds flew off into skies darkening
with winter dusk at three in the afternoon.

They're no more reasoning, our memories,
and no more ours than waxwings migrating
not randomly or wilfully but drawn
by the turning angles of the sun
and by the indecipherable code
implicit in the cells of brain and blood.
Memories come and go, not when we ask
but like the waxwings in the winter dusk.

The Chasm

They come from the same region as our dreams
and nightmares, from the far side of a time
barrier where mind's a microcosm
of wilds and tides and ways, across the chasm
into our minuted, intelligent
measuring of measured measurement
of time and light and space and blood and brain.

Or do I delude myself again?
Delusion may be a function of memory
but the state of mind isn't illusory
for we can trace the currents on our maps
of the brain... And trace the widening gaps
between brain and mind, the present and the past,
between our measured world and the world we've lost.

The Secret Life 1

To say they have a secret life is sheer
folly and yet I don't remember how
some came from out there to the here-and-now,
or now-and-then, of memory. Some veer
off course and cross, criss-cross mind's boundary
until memory dims to mere memory
of memory. Some of them disappear
completely from my mind; at least, I think
they do for when they cross the conscious brink
I can't be sure if they were ever here.
It seems a miracle I can recall –
through secrecy and doubt and the frontier
that's always changing – anything at all.
And the past is passing faster year by year.

The Secret Life 2

Unless I live to be a hundred and eight
or more, most of my life's already spent.
If I knew what some of the lost time meant
or if I thought life wasn't an accident
the future might not be too desolate
a territory, nor the journey's last
few stages so bewilderingly fast
as those I've travelled so far. The contrast
will be the less the more I can relate
the future to the past through memory.
But when I try to map those fifty-three
quick-as-a-flash fragmented years I see
the past is a province of the same state
as the future: new, unknown, inchoate.

The Republic

Rain lashed the West of Scotland Science Park.
The Rolls Royce pulled up on the new tarmac.
I sheltered underneath a whitebeam tree
and watched someone perform the ceremony
but can't remember who unveiled the plaque
or cut the ribbon. Princess? Prince? The Queen?

Odd details of that day displace the main
event in what at first seemed anarchy:
science, the social order, monarchy
were overrun. But now I know that rain
and wind and tree are all that I believe,
one involuntary hierarchy
of independent elements alive
in the republic of my memory.

The Mourners

Grief is a lesion. Networks in the mind
are ruptured, and the broken ends of thought
and fluttering hours come crowding round the wound.
The women carry flowers, bulbs and pot
plants, water, thick new candles in glass bells,
tins of polish for the metalwork –
the lattices of black wrought iron scrolls
around the graves – and little weeding forks
and hand trowels. The wound will never heal
completely but the kneeling women make
a quick unthinking task of death until
the agony of grief dulls to the ache
of time beginning again, and mind and life,
and grief becoming the memory of grief.

The Pact
(In Memoriam Neil Gunn, 1891–1973)

The many-coloured contours of the moor
were simplified into a long black ridge
and all the hollows between hill and shore
were filled with shadows. At the water's edge
he watched the wavering shoals of silver light
dull to a sullen sheen out in the bay,
where distances solidified as night
made a living darkness of the sky,
the moorland and the sea, the shingle beach.

The boy was shivering. The dark was near
enough to touch if he could only reach
through the closing circle of his fear.

He raised his hand; he brushed the creature's hide.
He sealed his pact with earth and air and tide.

The Victory
(In Memoriam Alexander Scott, M.C. 1920–1989)

'Done is a battle on the dragon black.'
You spoke as if the poets could win back
our nationhood, and the land's life or death
could be decided by the poet's breath:
Soutar, MacDiarmid, Henryson, Dunbar.

I pressed you once about your earlier war.
You waded through the dying and the dead
to reach the shore. Wounded, you would have bled
to death beside the men of your platoon
rather than give up the ground you'd won.

And when the enemy had you by the throat
at last, you joked in whispers and you fought
so long that by the end you'd found a way
of death that was another victory.

The Font
(In Memoriam Ronald West, 1934–1994)

You apologised for having grown so gaunt
that you were the living ghost of Ronald West.
You wanted us to see you were possessed
by peace as well as death. You didn't want
to see your ghost reflected in our eyes.
You were as gentle an apologist
for death as you had been a celebrant
of life and craftsmanship. You knew the font
that pressed words to the page and yet released
them into space. And you could civilise
the most barbarous texts with your imprint.
Dear visitant, I'm glad you've chosen to haunt
me for a time and help me recognise
the gift of goodness when a good man dies.

Voices

They left school at fourteen and went to work
in Grangemouth's soap factory, timber yards,
dockyards, ICI Dyestuffs – 'The Dyes';
at blackened iron foundries in Falkirk
and the aluminium smelter. When I heard
the way they greeted one another, 'Aye.
It's yursel, sir,' stopping in the street,
it was a challenge I could never meet.

I feared the voices of these patriarchs.
I listened to other voices, on the Third
Programme and Home Service, voices dark
with poetry, not dust. I aped the words
until the broadcast voices were ingrown
and this false, homeless accent was my own.

The Inheritance

The war, the hospitals – he was away
so long he was a stranger when he died;
I knew his face better from holiday
snapshots than from the life; and when I tried
to weep there were few tears. Later, I thought
I owed him part of my life for the years
he lost and for his early death. I ought
to have known that my father re-appears
in me no matter what I think: I feel
about books, craftsmanship, woodlands at dusk
just as he once did, his coded will
decoded as I sit here at my desk
translating impulses that might fulfil
my father's purpose and complete his task.

Trails

Part of the itinerary, that sense
of having wandered too far from the trail
across the hill? The January sun
was setting, the temperature falling and frost
grizzling the junipers. The mist grew dense
enough to cancel distances and chill
the sweet illusion dribbling down my spine.
I cursed myself, the journey and the cost
of it. And then – was it by simple chance
I found the other way across the hill?
Frost was re-focusing the stars and moon
so that I walked on light over the last
half-mile in a state of radiance
back into the world I thought I'd lost.

Ghost-hunter
for Susan Ambler

A poem doesn't exorcise its ghosts.
Instead, they pass at will across the coast
of conscious and unconsciousness to haunt
me with the same old fears and guilts. Ghosts won't
be bound, go by the book or treat a script
as something they must stick to. I accept,
willingly now, that even when I think
I've found words for a poem's missing links
they hover on the edge, only half-heard,
like the far cries of migratory birds.

I'm hunting for the creatures in the hope
that I may never fall into the trap
of catching them. The long hunt would be lost
if a poem wholly gave up its ghost.

ST. LOUIS
Jazz

ST. LOUIS
Jazz
·A HISTORY·

DENNIS C. OWSLEY

THE
History
PRESS

Published by The History Press
Charleston, SC
www.historypress.com

Front cover, top left: Photographer William P. Gottlieb. William P. Gottlieb Collection, Library of Congress, Washington D.C. Public domain; *top center*: Courtesy Western Historical Manuscript Collection, University of Missouri–St. Louis, UMSL Black History Project (1980–1983) Photograph Collection; *top right*: Photographer William P. Gottlieb. William P. Gottlieb Collection, Library of Congress, Washington, D.C. Public domain; *bottom*: Photograph by Bob Whiteside, with permission from Don Franz.
Back cover: Photographer Francis Wolff. Courtesy Mosaic Records Jazz Photography of Francis Wolff; *inset*: Photograph by Martin Schweig Studio, with permission from Asa Harris Finley.

First published 2019

Manufactured in the United States

ISBN 9781467141741

Library of Congress Control Number: 2019936992

*This book is dedicated to my late wife, Rosa, my present wife, Sara,
our six children and our seven grandchildren for putting up with my obsession.
Without family, we are nothing.*

CONTENTS

PREFACE

This book is, by necessity, a multimedia experience. A city that has an always-striving population has a lot of musicians and, since the early 1920s, has produced a lot of recordings—signposts that they have been here. The book is partially based on interviews. Normally, interviews are presented as excerpts to be read, but in this book, they are referenced to be heard by you, if you so desire. You, the reader, have a choice as to how much you want to dive into this history.

Whenever you come across a text that looks like this, [*Smith Interview*], you can follow this link to find that interview: https://www.stlpublicradio.org/jazz/city-of-gabriels/?rd=1.

Likewise, a listing of artist, recording title, tunes, date and recording company can get pretty boring, but if you read that one of your favorite artists issued a recording in 1998, you can have the choice of searching the complete online [*Discography*] for that artist. Use the link in the paragraph above and find the discography. It is a searchable .pdf file.

ACKNOWLEDGEMENTS

Thanks to my wife, Sara Serot, and Bob Klepper for proofing the documents in St. Louis. Thanks to Roscoe Crenshaw, Elise Wood, Ursula Oppens, Therese Dickman of the National Ragtime and Jazz Archive at Southern Illinois University–Edwardsville, the Western Historical Manuscript Collection, the Randle family and the Mercantile Library for providing photographs. Thanks to Paul DeMarinis for being a good friend and fellow scholar. A big thank-you to Terry Perkins, Michael Renner, Calvin Johnson and Dean Minderman for keeping the music before the public in the media.

INTRODUCTION

The early history of the music we call jazz is riddled with myths and false narratives that live on today. One of the things I want to accomplish with this book is to tell a coherent, true and fact-based story of jazz music in St. Louis all the way up to today. Here are some things that are said around St. Louis even today.

They say that jazz came up the Mississippi River to St. Louis and went to Chicago. Look at a map; the Mississippi goes to St. Paul, Minnesota, never a hotbed of jazz. The early jazz musicians moved around the country in trains, buses and cars.

They say that jazz broke out of New Orleans and came up the river to St. Louis in 1919, when Fate Marable brought Louis Armstrong and other New Orleans musicians to play on the steamer *J.S.* But Jelly Roll Morton was in St. Louis in 1914 and was living in Los Angeles in 1917. King Oliver was working in Chicago in 1918. How does this narrative fit with Fate Marable bringing the Paducah, Kentucky Jazz Band down the Ohio and Mississippi Rivers into New Orleans in 1918?[1]

They say that jazz is strictly an African American music. How does that fit with 32 percent of the nationally known early New Orleans trumpeters being white Italians? From the very beginning in St. Louis, black and white musicians were playing together out of the view of the authorities. In the 1920s, there were open band battles between black and white groups at establishments like Sauter's Park and Marigold Gardens.[2]

They say that jazz musicians were the poorest of the poor, but biographies of all the major jazz musicians show that the vast majority were firmly middle class and had some music lessons as children. They did not pick up instruments and just start playing this complex music.

They say that the music on the excursion boats that plied the Mississippi River around St. Louis was jazz. Eyewitness accounts by the musicians indicated that the boat captains bought stock arrangements of the hits of the day and the musicians had to play them exactly as written with no improvisation. These riverboats were known as "floating conservatories"; all the musicians, black and white, who spent any time on them continued their careers as "crack" readers when they left the boats.[3]

They say that Dixieland jazz is traditional jazz, played just like King Oliver and Jelly Roll Morton played it. But, research in the Tom Lord[4] discography and in photos of early New Orleans bands shows that tubas were not used in small combos until the 1927 Louis Armstrong Hot Seven. Dixieland began in San Francisco at the same time as the musical revolution known as bebop. It can be looked upon as a counterrevolution to that style. All the Dixieland combos began to use tubas, but they borrowed heavily from the bebop drumming style.[5]

St. Louis jazz is the result of the hard work of hundreds of musicians, people of substance who remained here or left for greater venues without the need for these myths.

Chapter 1

RAGTIME, RIVERBOAT EXCURSIONS AND THE BLUES

S t. Louis is somewhat unique because from 1895 until approximately 1920, it was a hotbed for two of the streams that coalesced into the music we call jazz: ragtime and blues. The places where these two music forms existed were, as was the custom of the Victorian era, known as "vice districts" or "sporting districts." The authorities looked the other way from the drunkenness, prostitution, gambling and drug use rampant in these districts. The ragtime district, known as Chestnut Valley, stretched from the site of today's Busch Stadium to east of Union Station. It was an entertainment area not only for the African Americans working the steamboats that went from New Orleans to St. Paul, but also for everybody else. The blues district, known as Deep Morgan, was, for a while, a separate district on Biddle Street located just north of where the Gateway Arch stands today [*Tichenor Interview*].

Several nationally known songs came from Chestnut Valley: "Frankie and Johnny" (about a lovers' quarrel in a Targee Street saloon) and two songs sung by "Mama Lou," a black entertainer at the well-known brothel known as the Castle, "Ta-Ra-Ra-Boom-De-Ay" (better known in the 1950s as "The Howdy Doody Song") and "There'll Be a Hot Time in the Old Town Tonight" (Sophie Tucker's theme song). According to Trebor Tichenor [*Tichenor Interview*], the moralists in St. Louis were constantly trying to shut down Chestnut Valley. A Catholic priest, Father Coffey, succeeded in getting a law passed forbidding piano playing in establishments where liquor was served. This was universally ignored, and Father Coffey was reassigned [*Tichenor Interview*].

We can make a good case that Tom Turpin, and not Scott Joplin, was the "King of Ragtime" in St. Louis. He published the first rag by an African American, "Harlem Rag," in 1898. He was the one in charge.[6] Turpin, a large man, played the piano at his Rosebud Bar standing up because it was set on blocks to accommodate his height. The Rosebud and the adjacent Hurrah Club were east of where Union Station stands today. The Hurrah Club was the gathering place for ragtime pianists such as Scott Hayden, Arthur Marshall, Joe Jordan and Louis Chauvin. Apparently, "cutting contests"—musical battles between local musicians and visiting musicians—happened at the Hurrah Club. These apparently led Turpin to sponsor ragtime piano contests at the Rosebud and later at the Booker T. Washington Theater, owned by his brother Charles, that later opened east of the Rosebud. The last contest was in 1916.

Scott Joplin apparently was in and out of St. Louis in the years 1885–94 and then moved, more or less permanently, to St. Louis in 1901 with his publisher, John Stark.[7] Joplin became associated with Turpin and apparently attended Hurrah meetings. He was the subject of a 1901 article in the *St. Louis Post-Dispatch* by the director of the St. Louis Choral Symphony Society, Alfred Ernst. This group was the predecessor of the St. Louis Symphony. There is no record of a Joplin performance in St. Louis, but he did record one piano roll, "The Strenuous Life," in St. Louis in 1902. Joplin recorded eighteen other piano rolls in the years 1901 to 1907, the time he lived in St. Louis. Joplin also filed a copyright application for a ragtime opera, *A Guest of Honor*, in 1903. He assembled a company and toured the country that same year. No copy of the score has been found.

John Stark published a number of classic rags that he orchestrated for brass bands. These were known as the *Red Backed Books* and brought about a new interest in ragtime when Gunther Schuller made a recording of some of them in a brass band setting [*Tichenor Interview*].

Joplin left St. Louis in 1907 and moved to Chicago and then New York, trying to find support for his opera *Tremonisha*, completed in 1910 and published in 1911. This opera encompassed a number of musical styles but was never performed in its entirety in his lifetime. It was performed in 1972. Joplin was posthumously awarded the Pulitzer Prize in 1976. He died from complications of syphilis on April 1, 1917.[8]

To many St. Louisans, its twentieth-century culture can be summed up in four things: the 1904 World's Fair, the St. Louis Cardinals, the Gateway Arch and Gaslight Square. An extraordinary amount of time is spent in the media on these four things. In this book, we will deal with two of them:

Left: Tom Turpin. *Right*: Scott Joplin. © *Scott Joplin State Historical Site, St. Louis.*

the 1904 World's Fair and Gaslight Square (in chapter 6). It is instructive to follow the city's fear of "low class" ragtime in the *Post-Dispatch* in the months of the run-up to the fair. The January 28, 1904 edition of the newspaper had the headline "No Ragtime—Will Take Away the Beauty of the Fair," said the "authorities." However, as long as the practitioner was white and "high class," it was all right to play ragtime at the fair. The *Post-Dispatch* of September 6, 1904, reported that New York socialite Dory Lyon put on a well-received "ragtime show" at the New York Pavilion. Another example of the power structure's dislike of ragtime was found in an article in the *Post-Dispatch* on February 17, 1915, excoriating pianist and bandleader Gene Rodemich for disturbing his fiancée's family by playing ragtime. The first mention of Rodemich was in the November 13, 1913 edition of the *Post-Dispatch*, where it was noted that he never played a song the same way twice.

In addition to the fair, there was a midway, where other, less "high class" amusements could be found. A lingering legend in St. Louis is that Scott Joplin performed there. He did not, because he was in Chicago [*Tichenor Interview*]. But ragtime was heard on the midway at the Spanish Café, and a beer hall called Old St. Louis presented the ragtime piano duo of Sam Patterson and Louis Chauvin. A number of tunes were composed for the fair, including "The Cascades" (Joplin), "St. Louis Rag" (Turpin), "On the Pike" (James Scott) and "St. Louis Tickle" (Theron C. Bennet). Two men who never attended the fair, Andrew B. Sterling and "Kerry" Mills, wrote the best-known song of the fair. It was "Meet Me in St. Louis," which was also the theme song of the 1944 film of the same name starring Judy Garland [*Tichenor Interview*].

By the time the World's Fair was over, ragtime was in decline in St. Louis. Most of the musicians went to Chicago and other midwestern cities. The Rosebud Bar closed in 1906 [*Tichenor Interview*]. Scott Joplin moved to Chicago and then to New York in 1907. The Scott Joplin House in St. Louis, where Joplin lived from 1901 to 1903 at 2658 Delmar Boulevard, is a Missouri State Historic Site and is open to the public.

What happened to ragtime? Ragtime is still played by people all over the world. Stephanie Trick, born in St. Louis, is a well-known and very good practitioner of the style. But ragtime, like nearly everything else, began evolving into two styles by 1910 or so. The two styles were "novelty piano" ("Kitten on the Keys," for example) and, more important, the "stride piano" style of the teens and 1920s that is the basis for the development of much of jazz [*Tichenor Interview*].

The musicians who stayed in St. Louis began working in the Deep Morgan area, north of where the Arch stands today, on Biddle Street. Musicians from the Mississippi Delta began migrating into the area. W.C. Handy, known as the "Father of the Blues," was in and out of St. Louis, notably in 1893, as he stopped on his way to Chicago for the upcoming World's Columbian Exposition there. Handy's earliest compositions were marketed as rags [*Tichenor Interview*]. The first edition of the sheet music of "St. Louis Blues" advertised it as a rag. It has a structure of a rag with two twelve-bar blues choruses, followed by a sixteen-bar bridge with a Spanish rhythm known as a "Habanera Rhythm" and closes with the twelve-bar blues structure. The "St. Louis Blues" is now the city's signature song and is the most recorded song in jazz. It has been recorded by jazz musicians a total of 2,188 times.[9]

Most people do not know that the first published blues was "Baby Seals Blues," by Frank "Baby" Seals (a vaudeville performer) and arranged by Artie Matthews, the music director of the Booker T. Washington Theater at the time. It was published in August 1912.[10] Handy's better-known composition, "Memphis Blues," was published two months later.

Things were happening on the riverfront other than freight moving up and down the Mississippi River into and out of St. Louis. Sometime before 1900, excursion steamers began taking customers on outings in the late spring, summer and early fall months. These excursions had bands playing the songs of the day. The excursions were racially segregated. Blacks were only allowed on the boats on Monday nights, a practice continued until 1969. By 1911, the Streckfus family was bringing freight and passengers to St. Louis from New Orleans, soon gaining a near monopoly on the Mississippi River steamboats. These steamboats were to have a lasting effect on jazz, bringing musicians into St. Louis and training them to be complete musicians on the "floating conservatories" they had become. Gene Rodemich's orchestra was one of the bands heard on the riverboats.

It is a good time to introduce Jesse Johnson.[11] He got his start as a dance instructor on the *Grey Eagle* excursion boat in 1913 and was promoting dances and cruises in St. Louis from 1915. He was an entrepreneur, building many businesses until his death in 1945. His family's businesses and promotions will be detailed in subsequent chapters of this book, along with an important event linked to the Johnson family that happened in Washington, D.C., in 2011.

Racial segregation of musicians and audiences led to the formation of two racially segregated unions at nearly the same time in 1896. A meeting with the labor organizer Samuel L. Gompers in Indianapolis with representatives from all the musicians' organizations in the country resulted in the formation of musicians' unions in the American Federation of Labor (AFL). In St. Louis, Local 2 represented white musicians who played in concert bands, the symphony and theater pit bands. Their black counterparts, represented by Local 44, played in small groups working in cabarets and at private parties and dances. The majority of customers on the riverboats, bawdy houses and circuses were white—both white and black segregated bands played for them. White musicians, however, did not play for black audiences. Both unions had the same work rules and wage scale.[12] This arrangement tenuously remained in place until the arrival of talking pictures. Every new technology brings disruption and displacement; the consequences of that particular technology shift will be discussed in chapter 3.

The *Argus* and the *Palladium* newspapers had advertisements for the black clubs and dance halls. Pythian Hall (at Lucas and Compton) was the major dance hall in the black community. Other establishments that employed black musicians were Bogg's Café (on Lawton), the Garden Café (Cardinal and Lawton), the Rathskeller Garden (Laclede and Leonard) and the Chauffeur's Club (on Pine). The major white dance hall was the Dreamland Ballroom (on Olive), with many mentions in the *Post-Dispatch* during this time. That establishment became the Arcadia Ballroom in 1925 and Tune Town in 1940 and burned to the ground in 1946.

Jelly Roll Morton was one of the more interesting musicians in jazz. He claimed to be the inventor of jazz and, among other things, was a con man. Morton came to St. Louis in 1914 and began to do well in "cutting contests" that were punctuated by his usual braggadocio. The St. Louis ragtime pianists tried to test Morton's skill by putting difficult pieces in the classical piano repertoire before him to see if he could read them at sight. He barely missed a note, holding back the fact that he had learned the pieces as a child and memorized them. When he told the local players about the con job, he was banished from the Chestnut Valley scene and went to South St. Louis, where the Germans lived.[13]

In addition to steamboat excursions, there was a burgeoning vaudeville scene in St. Louis at the Booker T. Washington, Odeon, Columbia and other theaters. Musicians were also working in cabarets, the names of which have been lost to history. There were also white and black community bands and dance bands that performed in parks and at private parties.

The Booker T. Washington Theater was owned by Tom Turpin's brother Charles. In 1916, a very surprising thing happened in racially segregated St. Louis. According to the *Argus*, the African American patrons of the Booker T. Washington Theater demanded more "high class acts," even if those acts were white. Thus, vaudeville was desegregated in St. Louis in that year. That venue was the site of a very interesting interracial concert in 1926.

One of the vaudeville acts that regularly visited the white and African American theaters and cabarets was the Creole Band.[14] It played in St. Louis and on the East Side six times from 1914 to 1917. This band was a pre-jazz band with the following personnel: New Orleans trumpet king Freddie Keppard, clarinetist George Baquet, trombonist Eddie Vincent, trumpeter Jimmy Paolo, guitarist Norwood Williams, bassist Bill Johnson and vocalist and dancer Henry Morgan Prince. Keppard had a productive career in Chicago in the 1920s, and Baquet recorded with Bessie Smith and Jelly Roll Morton. Bill Johnson had a long career with King Oliver's Creole Jazz Band, clarinetist Johnny Dodds and others. He lived to be one hundred years old.

Another one of the persistent legends in jazz is that Freddie Keppard recorded before the white Original Dixieland Jazz Band. The facts are that the Creole Band did record, but twenty-two months later. They made a test pressing for RCA Victor on December 2, 1918, that was never issued. By that time, the Original Dixieland Jazz Band had recorded thirty sides.[15] The

Post-Dispatch of April 16 and 17, 1917, contained ads for the first recordings by the Original Dixieland Jazz Band.

Over the years, there have been migrations of African Americans from the South to Chicago. One of these migrations happened in 1917 after World War I. The Illinois Central Railroad bypassed St. Louis. But some of these people did move to St. Louis and East St. Louis, Illinois. The major East St. Louis industry was meatpacking. As African Americans began coming into that city, fears were expressed in the *Post-Dispatch* that these were strike breakers waiting for the next strike to happen. These fears whipped up mob violence on May 28 and 29 and July 1, 2 and 3. All contemporary accounts in the *Post-Dispatch* in the aftermath place the blame squarely on the police. African Americans were stoned to death, shot and lynched. A piece in the July 3, 1917 edition detailed the horror of the riot. In a front-page headline, the July 4, 1917 edition of the *Argus* called it a "national disgrace." The black community in St. Louis has never forgotten the East St. Louis Race Riots that cost the lives of up to four hundred citizens and caused an estimated $400,000 in damage. They affected race relations in St. Louis for years to come.

Music making in this period in both white and black communities also took place in military-style community bands that served not only as entertainment but also as opportunities for instructing young musicians. The *Argus* listed the Harmony Club Band and Orchestra, the Blue and Harmony Band, the Odd Fellows Band, William Blue's Concert Band and the Knights of Pythias Band. All were active in the period from 1910 to 1919. Most of the well-known musicians in and from St. Louis in the 1920s went through these bands. Most of the major St. Louis African American brass players (trumpeters Dewey Jackson, Andrew "Big Babe" Webb, Shirley Clay, R.Q. Dickerson and Leonard "Ham" Davis; and trombonists Harvey Langford, Charles Lawson and Andrew Luper) came through the Odd Fellows Band, with Langford as the bandmaster. Another of the bandmasters was William Blue.[16] Through his son, clarinetist William Thornton Blue, he had an influence on Benny Goodman. Community bands in the black community of St. Louis continued to produce well-known jazz musicians through the 1950s.

A watershed was reached in the music scene in St. Louis when the black bandleader Fate Marable was sent by Captain John Streckfus to play solo piano opposite the white Gene Rodemich Orchestra in 1918. The next year, Marable brought an African American band to work on the steamer *St. Paul*. This band had Louis Armstrong and Norman Mason (trumpets), Davey

Jones (mellophone), Paul Dominguez (violin), Sam Dutrey (clarinet), Fate Marable (piano), George "Pops" Foster (bass) and Warren "Baby" Dodds (drums). The band was a sensation.[17] The July 30, 1919 edition of the *Post-Dispatch* had a story of an excursion for wounded World War I veterans on the steamer *J.S.* accompanied by music from a "Negro Jazz Band." Chapter 2 will discuss the changes in St. Louis music brought about by the arrival of these musicians.

Chapter 2

THE 1920s

BLUES, DANCE BANDS, JAZZ AND THE RADIO

In the 1920s, jazz in St. Louis was highly informed by the blues. A number of St. Louis jazz recordings had blues musicians in their personnel [*Discography*]. The area on Biddle Street known as "Deep Morgan" was the host to blues pianists like Speckled Red, Roosevelt Sykes, Wesley Wallace and Lonnie Johnson, who went on to New York and recorded with Louis Armstrong, Duke Ellington and the white guitarist Eddie Lang. Guitarists Big Joe Williams and Sylvester Weaver also worked in St. Louis.[18] A thriving blues scene was found in East St. Louis, with establishments like the Blue Flame Club, the 9-0-5 Club, Jim's Place, Boots on the Levee and Katy Red's. The latter club figured in Bix Beiderbecke's tenure in St. Louis in 1925. Two blues singers recorded in St. Louis: Victoria Spivey (in 1926) and a fourteen-year-old Helen Humes (in 1927) [*Discography*].

The riverboats in St. Louis and New Orleans loom large in the development of jazz, but not in the way that most people think. The musicians on these boats called them "floating conservatories," schools where musicians could learn and polish their craft. The bassist Pops Foster said that the performers played music to suit the Streckfus family, not the dancers. Each band had to learn, by sight, fourteen new numbers every two weeks who were picked by the Streckfus family.[19] The black bandleaders in 1920s St. Louis were Fate Marable, Charles Creath, Dewey Jackson, Eddie Allen and Floyd Campbell. Foster said that the Streckfuses made musicians out of a large number of people, including Louis Armstrong.[20] The white Gene Rodemich and Ted Jansen Orchestras also played on the excursion boats. Musicians who spent time on the riverboats finished their tenures as excellent sight readers.

Capitol steamer. *Streckfus Steamboats Advertisment, courtesy of the Mercantile Library at the University of Missouri, St. Louis.*

The real bandleaders on the boats were not the ones cited above but the Streckfus family. The people who fronted the bands were more like "straw bosses," musicians who rehearse a band, count off tempos and keep the musicians in line. In this world, the Streckfus people picked the music and dictated the tempos and durations of their performances. Rehearsals and performances were timed to the second. The Streckfus organization, not the straw bosses, paid the musicians.[21] This applied to both black and white bands. William Howland Kenney called them "hot dance bands."[22] These bands, in modern parlance, were cover bands, playing stock arrangements of the hits of the day note for note. Fate Marable made only two recordings in 1924, "Pianoflage" and "Frankie and Johnny" [*Discography*]. Neither of these sound like jazz, even by 1924 standards.

The notion that a "hot dance band" was a jazz band carried over into those who remember the swing era. George Simon's book *The Big Bands* lists more than four hundred big bands, but only a handful of them were in reality jazz bands.[23]

The riverboat customers were strictly segregated, with African Americans allowed on the boats only on Monday nights, but this did not apply to the Streckfus boats before 1920. Jesse Johnson and Charles Creath convinced the Streckfus brothers to allow blacks on their boats on Monday nights.[24] This segregated practice continued up to 1969. For excursions, the boats usually had black bands at night and white bands during the day. "Black Nights" on the boats were big social occasions, and everyone was dressed to the nines [*Hines Interview*].

Charles Creath Jazz-O-Maniacs (1924): Sammy Long (alto sax), William Rollins (tenor sax), Margie Creath (piano), Grant Cooper (trombone), Charles Creath (cornet) and Alexander Lewis (drums). © *SIUE Library and Information Services.*

Jesse Johnson nearly ended his career and his life in a May 1928 promotion. It was a battle of bands on the steamer *St. Paul* between the Alphonso Trent Orchestra (a very popular territory band that will be introduced in chapter 3) and the Floyd Campbell Band, fronted by Louis Armstrong. There was no attempt to limit the number of tickets. When the boat began to leave the dock, overloaded with five thousand fans, it began sinking. A return to the dock saved the day and many lives.[25]

Fate Marable (1890–1947) was born in Paducah, Kentucky. College educated, Marable played piano and a white man played violin on his job for the Streckfus family. Three other white musicians, very unusual for the time, expanded the band on the steamer *J.S.*, which went between Rock Island, Illinois, and New Orleans. Eventually, Marable brought his own Kentucky Jazz Band to New Orleans. He was sent to St. Louis in 1918 as an intermission pianist and brought Louis Armstrong and other New Orleans musicians to the city in 1919. Marable led riverboat bands until 1940 then worked until his death as a solo pianist at the Victorian Club in St. Louis.[26]

The decade of the 1920s was dubbed the "Roaring Twenties" by many observers, and Prohibition was the law of the land. This was the beginning of organized crime in the United States. Many of the speakeasies, clubs and ballrooms would not have existed without criminal connections. This was certainly true in St. Louis.

Segregation, organized crime, the riverboats, the burgeoning recording industry and the beginnings of radio were important in the development of jazz all over the country. St. Louis has no regional jazz style, because it was both a regional river shipping hub and a railroad hub, bringing in musicians of many different styles. These transportation modes also made it easy for many important musicians to leave St. Louis and gain international recognition.

From 1923 to 1928, St. Louis was a center for field recordings of many kinds of music by the Okeh, Vocalion, Brunswick and Victor labels, so we have a record of the many bands that worked in St. Louis during that time [*Discography*]. The field recordings ranged from preachers and boy-scout drummers to blues singers, jazz bands and just about anything that made a sound. Black and white jazz and dance bands were recorded. They came from all over the Midwest and included the Jesse Stone Blue Serenaders from St. Joseph, Missouri, and the King Oliver Dixie Syncopators in 1927. Both bands were very important in the history of jazz. A visiting Jelly Roll Morton (as Jelly Roll Martin) recorded "Soapsuds" in 1926 with a band that sounded like amateurs.

Because of the racial segregation that still exists in St. Louis, its jazz history consists of two parallel histories of black and white musicians that intersect only occasionally up to around 1950. Unfortunately, each history will have to be treated separately. In order to keep the histories in roughly chronological order, the white history will be treated first, because white players recorded first.

Elmer Schoebel, from East St. Louis, was a pianist who played in theaters and moved to Chicago in 1920. He was one of the first arrangers in jazz and made his first recordings with the New Orleans Rhythm Kings in 1922.[27]

A number of white dance bands also worked in St. Louis, most notably the Gene Rodemich Orchestra. He first recorded in 1919. That orchestra made a recording called "By the Pyramids" in 1921 with Frank Trumbauer on C-melody sax, playing a first in jazz: a series of breaks with alto saxophonist Bernie Kruger. Rodemich spent many seasons in the late 1910s and early '20s on the riverboats and theaters. Trumbauer was one of his star soloists.[28]

Rodemich was a St. Louisan born in 1890. A pianist, he was trained in the classics but was turned around by ragtime on the midway of the 1904 World's Fair. In 1909, he was the pianist on President William Howard Taft's Mississippi River tour. An article in the 1913 *Post-Dispatch* suggested that he was improvising in his performances. He accompanied vaudevillian Elise Janis on a tour of the front lines in World War I. Returning to St. Louis, Rodemich organized his first band in 1918. He had a big hit with "Swanee" in 1919. By 1926, Rodemich had left the boats and was playing in movie theaters, but he soon moved to Boston in 1926, then to New York. He began to play on the radio and died in 1934 as he began composing for films.[29]

Other white dance bands were recorded during this period. Some of the musicians in them played with Rodemich. These bands were the Arcadia Peacock Orchestra of St. Louis (1923, 1924), the David Silverman Orchestra (1924), Herbert Berger's Coronado Hotel Orchestra (1924, 1925) and Allister Wylie and his Coronado Hotel Orchestra (1928). Silverman and Wylie both played piano for Rodemich [*Discography*]. Rodemich's trombone player, Larry Conley, became a popular composer; "A Cottage for Sale" is his best-known composition. Clarinetist Pee Wee Russell got his professional start with the Berger Orchestra. The Ted Jansen Orchestra never recorded but was important for years.

A seven-piece band, Trimp's Ambassador Bell Hops, was recorded in May 1926 at Trimp's Ambassador Ballroom. Freddie Laufkoetter (trumpet) was involved with the musicians' union for many years. Vernon Brown (trombone) played with Benny Goodman and became a studio musician. Carl Maus (drums) played with Raymond Scott, Tommy Dorsey, Artie Shaw and Harry James.[30] The others on this recording were never heard from again. The ten-piece St. Louis Palladeo Orchestra recorded two sides for Okeh in October 1925. The personnel on these recordings is unknown, as is the Palladeo; no record of it exists in the archives of the *Post-Dispatch*. The Casa Loma Ballroom on Cherokee Street opened in 1927 and is still open for dancing.

Frank Trumbauer was born in Carbondale, Illinois, but was raised in St. Louis. He moved with his mother, a theater organist, to St. Louis in 1907. By 1920, Trumbauer was with Gene Rodemich. Trumbauer ran a classified ad in the February 22, 1920 *Post-Dispatch* advertising saxophone lessons and repair at his residence on Russell Boulevard. He worked with the Joe Kayser Band in 1921 and returned to St. Louis to partner with Ted Jansen. An ad in the September 1 edition of the *Post-Dispatch* shows their orchestra at Westminster Hall. He was with the Benson Orchestra in Chicago in 1923. In 1924, Trumbauer recorded a highly regarded solo on "San" with the Mound City Blue Blowers. That recording was widely admired by almost all saxophone players, black and white. He was the major influence on tenor saxophonist Lester Young.

Frank Trumbauer, New York, 1930. *Used with permission of William Trumbauer, Kansas City.*

Trumbauer then played with the Ray Miller Orchestra in 1925. With Miller, he played at the White House. Trumbauer accepted an offer to be a bandleader at the Arcadia Ballroom on September 28, 1925. He put together a band that included cornetist Bix Beiderbecke and clarinetist Pee Wee Russell, Ray Thurston (later Vernon Brown) (trombone), Bud Hassler (reeds) and others. They normally played opposite the Arcadian Serenaders with Wingy Manone (trumpet) and Sonny Lee (trombone). The Arcadian Serenaders made recordings for Okeh in 1924 and 1925. The Trumbauer band did not. It is known that the Trumbauer band also played at the Elks Club (with the Arcadian Serenaders) in Carbondale, Illinois, in 1926 and at Indiana University in Bloomington.[31]

When the Arcadia season was over on May 3, 1926, Beiderbecke, Russell and Trumbauer left for a job in Michigan. Trumbauer and Beiderbecke joined the Jean Goldkette Orchestra.

Vocalist Red McKenzie[32] had a long career as a vocalist into the 1940s, leading groups with varying personnel that he called the Mound City Blue Blowers. McKenzie used a comb with tissue paper and could get an uncanny imitation of a muted trumpet using this homemade instrument. He made one of the most famous recordings in jazz history with the Blue Blowers in 1929 on "Hello Lola" and "If I Could Be with You One Hour Tonight." The personnel on that recording included Glenn Miller (trombone), Pee Wee Russell (clarinet), Coleman Hawkins (tenor sax) and Gene Krupa (drums).

Charles Ellsworth "Pee Wee" Russell (1906–1969),[33] a member of the Trumbauer Arcadia Ballroom group, was an incorrigible person. He was born in Maplewood, Missouri, in 1906. His family moved to Muskogee, Oklahoma, where he began playing clarinet. A professional at age thirteen, he was sent to a military school in 1920, played in the band and was thrown out of the school in 1921. His family returned to St. Louis in 1922, and Pee Wee began playing day gigs on the riverboats. He left St. Louis in 1927, when his music showed his independent streak. He recorded with many musicians

Left: Dave Tough (*left*) and Pee Wee Russell, 1947. *Photographer, William P. Gottlieb. William P. Gottlieb Collection, Library of Congress, Washington, D.C. Public domain.*

Right: Red McKenzie. *Photographer, William P. Gottlieb. William P. Gottlieb Collection, Library of Congress, Washington, D.C. Public domain.*

playing in many styles, including a live 1963 performance with Thelonious Monk. His 1963 recordings include tunes by Monk, John Coltrane and Ornette Coleman. His last recording was with a modern big band arranged and conducted by St. Louisan Oliver Nelson. He became an abstract painter until his death.

Both the Okeh and Vocalion labels recorded African American blues and jazz bands in St. Louis. All of these recordings are documented in the *Discography*. The jazz bands were Charles Creath's Jazz-O-Maniacs (1925, 1926, 1927), Dewey Jackson's Peacock Orchestra (1925), Benny Washington's Six Aces (1925), the Old St. Louis Levee Band with Jelly Roll "Martin" (1926), Powell's Jazz Monarchs (1926) and Oliver Cobb's Rhythm Kings (1929).

The Cab Calloway Orchestra can trace its roots to St. Louis. In 1923, Wilson Robinson organized a band in the city composed of musicians from Kansas City and St. Louis.[34] The band played in vaudeville for a season on both coasts. It ended up at the famed Cotton Club in New York two years before Duke Ellington started working there. Trumpeter Louis Metcalf left St. Louis with this band. Leadership of the band eventually changed over to violinist Andrew Preer. It recorded as the Cotton Club Orchestra in 1925

Dewey Jackson and His Musical Ambassadors, 1921. *Courtesy of Dan Vernhettes, Paris, France.*

The Missourians, 1930. Cab Calloway (baton), William Thornton Blue (alto sax, in center). *Courtesy of Mark Beresford, London.*

and again as the Missourians in 1929. St. Louis clarinetist William Thornton Blue is heard on the latter recordings. The band became the Cab Calloway Orchestra in 1930.[35]

In the early 1920s, four St. Louis musicians left the city and eventually ended up with Fats Waller.[36] Trumpeter Leonard "Ham" Davis left for New York in 1925 and eventually recorded with the McKinney Cotton Pickers and with the Chocolate Dandies in 1929. Waller played piano on both of these recordings. Davis also recorded with Fats Waller and His Buddies, Eddie Condon and the Charlie Johnson Orchestra, also in 1929. Davis was in demand in the 1930s, playing with Louis Armstrong and others.[37]

The Harris family of Arville Harris (reeds) and his brother Leroy Harris Sr. (banjo) recorded with Clarence Williams and King Oliver in New York throughout the 1920s. Arville played with Waller in 1929. Leroy Harris Jr. was a reed player who worked with Earl Hines in the 1930s and '40s.[38] He also played with Singleton Palmer in St. Louis.

Reed player Emmett Matthews (1902–?) left St. Louis in 1923 with Wilson Robinson's band. From 1928 until 1931, he worked with Bill Benford's band, which became Fats Waller's Rhythm. Matthews worked with Waller until 1937[39] and then worked in theater orchestras until the 1950s.

Eugene "Honey Bear" Sedric is a graduate of the Knights of Pythias band. In 1922, he played on the riverboats with Charles Creath, Fate Marable and Dewey Jackson. He also left in 1923 and went to New York. Sedric worked with Ed Allen and Sam Wooding (who took him to Europe) before joining Waller in 1934, where he remained until 1942. He then worked in New York and Europe until 1961, when he retired due to failing health [*Discography*].

Saxophonist Jerome Pasquall (1902–1971) grew up in St. Louis and played mellophone in the Odd Fellows Band. Pasquall was in the army in World War I and then came home, playing clarinet after his discharge. He played with Ed Allen's Whispering Gold Band in 1919 and, in St. Louis, played with Marable and Creath. He left the city in 1924 and played with Doc Cook's Dreamland Orchestra in Chicago and with Fletcher Henderson and other bands.[40] He never returned to St. Louis.

Gene Sedric, 1947. *Photographer, William P. Gottlieb. William P. Gottlieb Collection, Library of Congress, Washington, D.C. Public domain.*

As St. Louis was both a north–south and an east–west transportation hub, musicians stranded while on the road could find work with other traveling bands moving through the area. In 1927, King Oliver formed a new version of his Dixie Syncopators, played a few jobs on the SS *Capitol* and left for New York. While in St. Louis, they recorded "Black Snake Blues" [*Discography*].

In jazz, St. Louis is known for a series of powerful trumpet players. According to Judge Nathan Young, the trumpet teachers from the turn of the last century were German, and the early black trumpet players took lessons from them [*Young Interview*]. St. Louis trumpet players were influenced by the German brass bands. Early New Orleans trumpet players had a wide vibrato, which narrowed in St. Louis and narrowed even further in Davenport, Iowa (Bix Beiderbecke). David Hines described the St. Louis trumpet as being clear and singing, with bent notes derived from the human voice singing the blues [*Hines Interview*].

There was another influence on the early trumpeters: Joseph Gustat, who was the principal trumpet player in the St. Louis Symphony. Gustat had a music store serving both white and black customers. According to Clark Terry, he recommended a Heim mouthpiece, a very thin but very deep mouthpiece. Apparently, at one time, most all the trumpet players used this mouthpiece [*Terry Interview*].

The list of St. Louis trumpet players who belong to the evolution of this sound is long. Charles Creath, Dewey Jackson and Oliver Cobb never left St. Louis. Cobb was being groomed to replace Louis Armstrong on the Brunswick label when he drowned in 1930 [*Palmer Interview*]. Ed Allen recorded with Bessie Smith and Clarence Williams. Louis Metcalf, Shorty Baker and Clark Terry all played and recorded with Duke Ellington and many others.[41] Irving "Mouse" Randolph played with many major big bands. Leonard "Ham" Davis played with the Charlie Johnson Orchestra, and Eddie Condon performed with Jack Teagarden, the Chocolate Dandies and McKinney's Cottonpickers.[42] Joe Thomas was one of the top studio trumpet players in New York in the 1940s.[43] Miles Davis changed the course of twentieth-century music at least four times.[44] Baikida E.J. Carroll now writes theater music (see chapter 7). Lester Bowie's highly original music was heard with the Art Ensemble of Chicago, his own Brass Fantasy and New York Organ ensemble (see chapter 7). Russell Gunn successfully combines hip-hop beats and jazz (see chapter 9), and Keyon Harris can be heard in a variety of contexts, in pop, jazz and films, including Don Cheadle's biopic of Miles Davis (see chapter 10).

Joe Thomas, 1947. *Photographer, William P. Gottlieb. William P. Gottlieb Collection, Library of Congress, Washington, D.C. Public domain.*

Charles Creath was born in Ironton, Missouri, in 1896.[45] According to David Hines [*Hines Interview*] and Clark Terry [*Terry Interview*], he was the "Godfather" of St. Louis trumpet playing. His parents moved to East St. Louis when he was fourteen. Creath went to high school there and was adept at many woodwind, brass and keyboard instruments. After two years with the Ringling Bros. Circus, he moved home in 1919, organizing his band, the Jazz-O-Maniacs, the same year. Creath played in all venues, including the Streckfus steamers. He was a favorite in the Italian neighborhood known today as "The Hill." He was the first black band booker in St. Louis and would book three or four bands under his name, driving his Marmon car between gigs to play a few numbers with each band. Creath contracted tuberculosis in 1928 and had to stop playing wind instruments. He led bands on the riverboats, playing mostly accordion, and moved to Chicago, worked in the defense industry in World War II and committed suicide in 1951 [*Creath V Interview*].

Creath was a gambler and played with his employees' salaries. It was always a question whether you would get no pay or an increased salary. Creath's Jazz-O-Maniacs recorded two sides that included "Market Street Blues" on December 2, 1924. In 1925, the same group recorded six sides. Creath made his last two recordings in 1927 with a ten-piece group [*Discography*]. William Thornton Blue (clarinet) was heard on all of the Creath sides. The 1925 recordings had a white trombonist, Sonny Lee, who played at the Arcadia Ballroom.

An important sidelight to Creath's career was his friendship with the white bandleader Ted Jansen and his musicians. They staged interracial band battles at Marigold Gardens in South St. Louis, at Creve Coeur Lake Park and at the Westlake Dance Pavilion.[46]

Trumpeter Dewey Jackson (1900–1963) was also important in leading bands on the riverboats and working in cabarets in St. Louis. His nickname was "squirrel" [*Terry Interview*], and he was the loudest trumpet player the St. Louis musicians had ever heard [*Palmer Interview*]. He played with Charles Creath in 1919 and again in 1924 and led his own bands under different names from 1920 to 1923. He joined Andrew Preer's Cotton Club Orchestra in New York and returned via New Orleans. Until the end of the riverboats, Jackson worked with Marable or led his own bands. Vertna Saunders, a trumpeter in the 1930s, described Jackson's playing as "looking like it was the last thing he would ever do."[47]

Trumpeter Andrew "Big Babe" Webb never left St. Louis. He recorded the "Compton Avenue Blues" in 1925 with drummer Benny Washington's Six Aces. The July 26, 1926 *Post-Dispatch* has Washington's Six Aces listed as playing on both the *J.S.* and the *St. Paul*. Banjo player Pete Patterson ("Banjo Pete") worked with the Aces and many other St. Louis bands well into the 1970s [*Discography*].

Trumpeter and vocalist Oliver Cobb's playing resembled Louis Armstrong so much that he was being groomed to replace Armstrong on the Brunswick label [*Palmer Interview*]. His group, the Oliver Cobb Rhythm Kings, recorded in Chicago in 1929, playing a risqué tune, "The Duck's Yas-Yas-Yas," and one other [*Discography*]. Pianist James "Stump" Johnson, brother of Jesse Johnson, composed the tune. Apparently, he never obtained a copyright, because a group called the Three Peppers stole it and had a hit record with it in the 1930s. The pianist in the Rhythm Kings was Edith Johnson, wife of Jesse Johnson. Singleton Palmer, a star on Gaslight Square, made his recording debut on these sides. Palmer's career will be covered more extensively in subsequent chapters.

Cobb recorded again in 1930 in Grafton, Wisconsin, in a duet with Edith Johnson [*Discography*]. By 1929, pianist Eddie Johnson had taken over the piano chair of the Rhythm Kings. Chapter 3 will have more on Cobb and Eddie Johnson.

St. Louis in the 1920s had a number of very good musicians in addition to its trumpet players. Clarinetist and saxophonist William Thornton Blue (1902–1968), the son of bandleader William Blue, left with Wilson Robinson in 1923 but soon was back playing with Creath and Jackson. The director of jazz studies at Webster University, Paul DeMarinis, remarked that Blue was in the same league as Johnny Dodds.[48] He left again to play with the Cotton Club Orchestra and then to tour Europe with Noble Sissle. Blue came off the road in New York in 1929 and recorded with the Missourians. Rex Stewart claimed that Benny Goodman's growl sound came from Blue. Later, he recorded with Louis Armstrong and Cab Calloway and played in many bands and jam sessions. His mental health began to fail, and by 1935, he was institutionalized at the Marlboro Psychiatric Hospital until 1940. He spent the rest of his life in the New Jersey State Mental Hospital, dying in 1968.[49]

Born in St. Louis, saxophonist William Rollins (1901–1971) went through the Odd Fellows Band and worked with Creath and in other bands on the riverboats in the 1920s. Following that, he worked with George Hudson and Buggs Roberts. As World War II was approaching, Rollins organized the Scullin Steel Band in 1941. He was active in the musicians' union for over thirty years.[50]

Sammy Long (1901–?) was a saxophonist who worked with the Creath (1920–1925), Dewey Jackson (1925–26), Floyd Campbell (1928–30) and Harvey Langford bands on the riverboats until 1934.[51]

Drummer Harry Dial (1907–1987) was a professional musician by the age of fourteen. Playing gigs at the Manchester Café, the Manhattan Café and the Almac Hotel while he was still in school, he eventually joined Fate Marable on the *J.S.* Dial was soon playing all over St. Louis with Charles Creath, Dewey Jackson, Norman Mason and Jimmy Powell. In 1928, he moved to Chicago and in 1933 went on to New York. He worked with Louis Armstrong and was a member of Fats Waller's Rhythm from 1934 to 1935. Dial stayed active in music until around 1980. He also wrote a delightful autobiography.[52]

Trumpeter John "Buggs" Hamilton (1911–1947) moved to New York in 1930. He played with Chick Webb and with Kaiser Marshall in 1935. Hamilton was with Waller from 1928 to 1942. In 1943, he contracted tuberculosis and died in St. Louis in 1947.[53]

Jazz is unusual for an underappreciated reason. It may be the institution closest to a true meritocracy in the world. If you can play, you are in the family. Social, economic or racial status does not matter, only one's playing ability. Its early history has many instances of black and white musicians getting together after hours, out of sight of the authorities, jamming and exchanging ideas. St. Louis was no exception to that. We mentioned as examples the Booker T. Washington Theater desegregating its stage in 1916 and the battles of bands between Ted Jansen and Charles Creath. Other examples will follow.

In this period, a number of clubs and cabarets in the black community had music.[54] Some of them were as follows: the Hummingbird (at Compton and Lucas), Jazzland (on Market), the Wedge Club (on Olive), the Piccadilly (Sixth and Chestnut) and the Paradise Dance Palace (on Sarah). One club, the Chauffeur's Club on West Pine, stood out for years. The club had its own house band, Powell's Jazz Monarchs. There are two Jimmy Powells in jazz. The more famous one was born in 1914 (as per Wikipedia) and had a long career in jazz. The bandleader at the Chauffeur's Club would have been twelve years old when the group recorded two sides in 1926. There were integrated after-hours jam sessions at the club for years.[55]

The New Orleans bassist Pops Foster recalled that during the period of the Frank Trumbauer Band engagement at the Arcadia Ballroom, Bix Beiderbecke and Pee Wee Russell rented an apartment in Granite City, Illinois. Mondays were the musicians' day off, and all the musicians, black and white, went over there and partied until dawn.[56] So it was no surprise that, according to Zutty Singleton, Beiderbecke, Russell and possibly Trumbauer played with the Charles Creath band at a benefit on the integrated stage of the Booker T. Washington Theater in 1926.[57]

The period from 1920 to 1926 was one of experimentation for the new entertainment medium of radio. By 1926, there were a number of about one-hundred-watt radio stations, some of which were sharing the same frequency with different air times. In St. Louis jazz, WIL and WEW were presenting jazz bands into the 1930s. The January 7, 1926 edition of the *Post-Dispatch* listed the Gene Rodemich Orchestra. The April 23, 1927 edition listed Charles Creath's Jazz-O-Maniacs, and on May 27, Benny Washington's Six Aces was advertised on WIL. The 1930s and '40s was the period of the greatest number of appearances by local bands. These will be detailed in chapters 3 and 4. Radio represented a technological shift that was good for St. Louis musicians, in that it gave them more exposure around town.

Chapter 1 of this book detailed the arrangement between blacks (Local 44) and whites (Local 2) for the division of labor. Like all agreements between a majority and a minority culture, the arrangements were subject to change at the whim of the majority culture. This division of labor ceded the movie theater jobs to Local 2. This tenuous arrangement between Locals 2 and 44 began to fracture in 1927, when talking pictures arrived. With this technological shift, Local 2 jobs in the movie theaters disappeared. Local 2 members began agitating to take Local 44's jobs. An example of a technological shift that was not helpful to both locals finally broke out into a one-sided war on Local 44 in the 1930s. This is detailed in chapter 3.

By 1929, the gathering storm of wild speculation in the stock market came crashing down on the country. This led to the Great Depression of the 1930s. Hard times were ahead for all, but our black citizens especially suffered during this period.

Chapter 3

HARD TIMES IN ST. LOUIS

T he Great Depression, which started in late 1929 and lasted until the beginning of World War II, was very rough on people and businesses. The St. Louis recovery took longer than cities of a similar size. Manufacturing losses were worse in 1939 (57 percent of the 1929 level), while the national number was 84 percent of the 1929 level. By 1933, unemployment in St. Louis was over 30 percent, with 80 percent of black residents unemployed or underemployed.[58] It was common to fire black workers and replace them with whites. Whites got pay raises; blacks did not. Organized labor excluded blacks from the skilled and building trades. The one exception was the hod carriers' union.[59]

This effort to disenfranchise minorities extended to the musicians' unions, with the white union (Local 2) in a one-sided war against the black union (Local 44). In 1931, the charter of Local 2 was revoked, a result of the lies and chicanery of Local 2 since the technology shift of 1927. The black musicians entered a situation close to involuntary servitude. Similar racist behavior was involved with musicians' unions in Kansas City, Denver and San Francisco. Musicians in Kansas City would not accept being disenfranchised, while those in San Francisco sued the white union.

In St. Louis, the black musicians kept working, often at non-union scale. One thing in their favor was that the mobsters who ran the clubs liked the black musicians and their music. According to "Lyge" Shaw and Eddie Randle, there were only three working white dance bands in St. Louis in the early 1930s: Ted Jansen, Lou Chortcot and Harry Lang. From the first day of the charter revocation, blacks worked to get their union back. Drummer "Lyge" Shaw spearheaded the effort and succeeded in 1944, much of it at his own personal expense, when Local 197 was formed. The two unions remained segregated until 1971.[60] The forced re-integration of the two unions will be discussed in chapter 7.

During this period, a number of ballrooms and cabarets catered to white and black customers. Ads in the *Post-Dispatch* seem to place both groups in the venues on different nights. As the Depression began to lift, all of these venues started booking midwestern territory and national swing bands. These venues were the Casa Loma, Castle, Grotto and Tune Town Ballrooms. Forest Park Highlands in 1939 also presented national bands. The Arcadia Ballroom advertised in this period but did not mention musicians or bands. Examples of visiting national swing bands in the 1930s are Jan Garber, Kay Kyser, Count Basie, Clyde Lucas and Fletcher Henderson at the Casa Loma; Ella Fitzgerald, Erskine Hawkins, McKinney's Cotton Pickers, Blue Baron and Andy Kirk at Forest Park Highlands; Frank Trumbauer at Tune Town; and Paul Whiteman and Duke Ellington at the Coronado Hotel.

In addition, local musicians played these venues, but their appearances were apparently not well advertised. The Castle Ballroom had Dewey Jackson's Musical Ambassadors and the Charles Creath band several times. The Casa Loma and the Arcadia Ballroom advertised the Tony DiPardo Orchestra in a double bill with Ludwig's Accordion Band. A poster for the black fraternity Chi Sig's Black Ball at the Arcadia in 1937 was found on the Internet. Some other venues were Sauter's Park, Westlake Park, Gray's Grove, the Missouri Hotel, the Aragon, the Mission Theater and the Bridge-Head Inn.

On August 25, 1932, Club Plantation opened at Delmar and Enright. The club was owned and managed by mobster "Big Tony" Scarpelli and his brother James. It was modeled after New York's Cotton Club, with an all-black staff and black musicians and entertainers. Kimball Dial claimed that the Plantation was planned to be a racially mixed establishment but that the idea was quashed by an ultimatum from the police.[61] The first band was the Rupe Floyd Band out of Illinois. Eddie Johnson's Crackerjacks came next, followed by a band led by trumpeter Walter "Crack" Stanley that broadcast over KWK radio. In 1934, the Jeter-Pillars Orchestra began a long residency as the house band that lasted until 1944.

Some alumni of this band were trumpeter Harry "Sweets" Edison, guitarists Charlie Christian and Floyd Smith, tenor saxophonist Jimmy Forrest, arranger Tadd Dameron, bassists Walter Page and Carl Pruitt and drummers Kenny Clarke, "Big" Sid Catlett and Jo Jones, all of whom became very well known internationally.[62] Trumpeter George Hudson, a bandleader and teacher in St. Louis for many years, was recruited from Kansas City in 1936 [*Hudson Interview*]. The further adventures of this band will be detailed in chapter 4.

The Plantation was a "set-up" club where the patrons brought their own liquor and the Plantation sold them mixers and food. This apparently was a ploy to get around closing times for establishments that sold liquor. But in the October 25, 1933 edition of the *Post-Dispatch*, Big Tony was charged with violating the closing laws.

Jesse Johnson and his brother James "Stump" Johnson and their families had an effect on St. Louis culture for decades. Jesse started as a dance instructor on excursion boats and moved to promoting black bands on the boats. By the end of the 1920s, he had the city sewed up. Any nationally known black band had to go through him. When he brought a name band into St. Louis, he increased ticket sales by having one or more local bands

Club Plantation floorshow. © *Western Historical Manuscript Collection, St. Louis.*

"battle" them. He promoted Cab Calloway and Duke Ellington by dropping leaflets from airplanes. Calloway had a crowd of over eighteen thousand in the Arena at the height of the Depression. Johnson desegregated Forest Park Highlands by bringing in national bands and adding St. Louis bands to the bill [*Dixon Interview*].

Over the years, Jesse Johnson also owned a number of businesses, including a record shop, a cab company and a restaurant. Johnson branded all of these businesses with the name "Deluxe." The Deluxe Café's impact on jazz will be discussed at the end of this chapter.

James "Stump" Johnson continued to work in clubs, as a policeman and as manager of the Deluxe Café until his death in 1969. "Stump" had a son, Harry E. Johnson, a lawyer who became president and CEO of the Martin Luther King Jr. Memorial Project Foundation. The King memorial statue in Washington, D.C., was dedicated on October 11, 2011.

Eddie Johnson, an aggressive businessman, was in the piano chair of Oliver Cobb's Rhythm Kings. According to the May 31, 1930 edition of the *Post-Dispatch*, they played on KMOX. An article in the May 25 edition claimed the band had just returned from playing the Cotton Club in New York. Soon after this radio appearance, Cobb drowned in the Mississippi. He was an epileptic and apparently had a seizure. Eddie Johnson took over the band and renamed it Eddie Johnson's Crackerjacks [*Johnson Interview*]. The Crackerjacks recorded for Victor in 1931, playing "The Duck's Yas-Yas-Yas" and "Good Old Bosom Bread" [*Discography*]. Trumpeter Harold "Shorty" Baker, who went on to stardom with Duke Ellington, was in the band.

A well-known alto saxophonist, Tab Smith, came into St. Louis to play with Dewey Jackson. Eddie Johnson eventually raided the group for Smith and several other musicians. That broke up Jackson's band and led to the departure of the Crackerjacks' entire horn section. Johnson recruited more St. Louis musicians, formed a big band and called it Eddie Johnson's Victor Recording Orchestra. Ironically, Johnson never recorded again. Alto saxophonist Don Stovall left and ended up in New York, playing with Cootie Williams, Pete Johnson and Red Allen. The other saxophonist, Kimball "Cabbage Head" Dial, remained in St. Louis. Eddie Johnson eventually moved to New York, opened his own booking office and booked his own bands [*Johnson Interview*].

Born in Villa Ridge, Illinois, Eddie Randle (1905–1997) came from a musical family. His grandfather and uncle were musicians. He learned to read musical notation via "shape notes," an older system. Randle began playing trumpet at seventeen. He came to St. Louis in 1923. Primarily

Eddie Johnson's Crackerjacks. © *Western Historical Manuscript Collection, St. Louis.*

self-taught, his only musical job before he formed his band was with Warner Long. He was also the band booker. He formed his band, the St. Louis Blue Devils, in 1932 and never looked back. Randle found that the band could make more money playing one-nighters all over the Midwest, gaining his bookings because people in the little towns heard his twice-weekly noon broadcasts on WEW. His band went to Sodus Point, New York (1939 and 1941); Stevens Point, Wisconsin (1936); and Dubuque, Iowa (1937) [*Randle Interview*].

From 1943, Randle only sporadically led bands, until 1964. He was a full-time funeral director nearly up until his death. Miles Davis is his most famous alumnus, but other alumni of the Blue Devils include trumpeters Clark Terry, "Sleepy" Tomlin and David Hines; saxophonists Jimmy Forrest, Ernie Wilkins, Oliver Nelson, Charles Pillars and Willie Akins; trombonist

St. Louis Blue Devils in Forest Park, St. Louis, early 1930s. *Used with permission of the Eddie Randle family, St. Louis.*

Druie Bess; pianist Tommy Dean; and bassist Jimmy Blanton. Wilkins and Nelson began their arranging careers with him. He was also a philosopher and teacher and the wisest man the author has ever known.

The horn section that broke away from Eddie Johnson formed a band they called the Original St. Louis Crackerjacks (because of Eddie Johnson's Crackerjacks). By this time, pianist Chick Finney was leading the band. They were on WEW from 1935 to 1939 and recorded seven sides in Chicago in 1937 [*Discography*]. The trumpeter playing the beautiful solo on "Echo in the Dark" is thought to be Levi Madison. According to Clark Terry, Madison had one of the most beautiful trumpet sounds he ever heard [*Terry Interview*]. Miles Davis was an early admirer of Madison. For some reason, this band never broke out of St. Louis.

The other black bands and bandleaders in St. Louis—Charles Creath, Dewey Jackson, Fate Marable and Harvey Lankford—did not record during the Depression, so we do not know very much about their specific personnel. We do know that they were active in the dance halls and other venues listed earlier and on the riverboats during the Depression, with many engagements advertised in the *Post-Dispatch*. Kimball Dial described a band led by trumpeter Walter "Crack" Stanley that lasted for a year at Club Plantation. It was heard over KWK.[63]

The black riverboat musicians included trumpeters Walter "Crack" Stanley, Louis Eckhardt, "Sleepy" Tomlin, Vertna Saunders and Clifford King; reed players Sammy Long, Earl Carruthers, Kimball Dial, Horace Millinder and Joe Neville; trombonists Harvey Lankford, James Beard, Robert Carter and Willie Austin; and pianists Gus Perryman, Burrowes Lovingood and Robert Bell.[64] Apparently, solos were permitted in the Lankford band.

The white bands were led by Harry Lang, Ted Jansen, Lou Chortcot, Dewey Brockmeyer and Charlie Booth. They did not record and apparently did not work on the riverboats.

A band sponsored by the Works Progress Administration (WPA) worked all over St. Louis and proved to be a lifeline for the musicians. Some of the best musicians and entertainers worked in the band, which included a symphony orchestra. The musicians were paid for both rehearsals and performances.[65]

Another black band was very important in the development and training of musicians. It was neither a jazz band nor a dance band but a drum-and-bugle corps sponsored by the Tom Powell American Legion Post. Eddie Randle's father started it [*Randle Interview*]. Many well-known St. Louis musicians played in that band, which won a Missouri State Championship in 1935. The corps was still training musicians in the early 1950s. In the 1930s, Clark Terry, who fondly remembered winning that championship, Charles Fox (Dexter Gordon, Sonny Criss, Jimmy Forrest and others) and bassist Arvell Shaw (Louis Armstrong) all trained in the corps [*Terry Interview*].

We have mentioned some engagements by St. Louis musicians on the radio, a staple for the entertainment of people who were essentially broke and could not go out to restaurants and cabarets. The *Post-Dispatch* radio logs give a fairly good picture of jazz and dance bands on the air in the city during the Depression. We have presented the Oliver Cobb broadcasts on KMOX earlier in this chapter. Eddie Johnson broadcast regularly on KMOX for several years, serving as its house band. Dewey Jackson's Musical Ambassadors were heard on WIL in several broadcasts in 1931. We have mentioned the St. Louis Blue Devils on WEW twice weekly at noon from 1933 to 1936. The St. Louis Crackerjacks had a regular broadcast on WEW from 1935 to 1939. The Jeter-Pillars Orchestra was on KMOX in 1936. As the country began recovering from the Depression, broadcasts of national bands increased. So, beginning in 1936, Cab Calloway, Duke Ellington, Benny Goodman, Fletcher Henderson, Count Basie and Earl Hines were heard on the radio in St. Louis. Tommy Dorsey was heard in 1937, along with local bands.

One curiosity was a show called *Harlem Rhythm* on WIL. It began near the end of 1933 and was obviously quite popular because it lasted until 1941. All the data indicate that it was a local show and not a network show. There is no listing of it in the New York radio logs. Miles Davis and pianist Ralph Sutton recalled hearing Fats Waller on the show, inspiring both of them in different ways. We do not know the source of the music. It had to be either phonograph records or network airchecks.

Musicians came and left St. Louis during the Depression. Trombonist Druie Bess was born in Montgomery City, Missouri, in 1901. He worked around the Midwest until he joined Jesse Stone's Blue Serenaders in St. Joseph. This band recorded in St. Louis in 1927, recording two solos that were considered advanced for the time. Eddie Randle recruited him in 1935. During his time in St. Louis, Bess played with all the St. Louis black bands up to 1944. He then spent two years with Earl Hines. After other musical jobs, Bess returned to St. Louis in 1948.[66]

St. Louis–born Harold "Shorty" Baker was originally a drummer but switched to trumpet. Baker worked with Fate Marable in 1930 and went to Chicago, returning in 1932 to play and record with Eddie Johnson. After this band broke up, Shorty and his trombonist brother, Winfield, remained with the original Crackerjacks. Shorty left in 1936 to join Don Redman and then Duke Ellington (1938), Teddy Wilson (1939) and Andy Kirk (1940–42). He was married to Kirk's pianist, Mary Lou Williams, for a time. In 1942, Baker rejoined Ellington and remained with him until 1952, interrupted by military service in 1944. He then freelanced in New York until his death in 1966.[67]

Trumpeter Clark Terry, one of the great trumpeters and humanitarians in jazz history, was born to a poor family in Carondelet in 1920. At an early age, he constructed a "trumpet" from a water hose with a funnel on one end. His sisters raised him after his mother died in 1926. His brother-in-law Cy Mackfield played tuba with Dewey Jackson. Terry's first instrument at Vashon High School was a valve trombone, and he was taught by Clarence Hayden Wilson's assistant, Leonard Smalls. He also talked with Joseph Gustat about technique. In high school, he played at the Lincoln Theater on Market Street. After high school, Terry traveled with Willie Austin's band in the Reuben and Cherry Carnival for a year. Returning to St. Louis, he worked with Bennie Reed, a one-legged piano player, and played occasional jobs with Eddie Randle and Jackson [*Terry Interview*]. Chapter 4 will continue his story.

Don Stovall was an alto saxophonist who was born in St. Louis in 1913. He played with Dewey Jackson, Fate Marable and Eddie Johnson on the boats before leaving for Chicago in 1936.[68]

One of the pioneering electric guitarists in jazz, Floyd Smith was born in St. Louis in 1917.[69] He worked with the usual St. Louis riverboat bandleaders in the 1930s. While he was with the Jeter-Pillars Orchestra in 1937, they recorded four sides, including their theme, "Lazy Rhythm." Smith's electric guitar solos preceded those of Charlie Christian by two years.[70] He had a hit, "Floyd's Guitar Blues," with Andy Kirk six months before Christian made his first commercial recording. Smith moved permanently to Indianapolis in 1944.

Trumpeter Karl George, born in St. Louis in 1913, began his career with Warner Long and then moved through many bands and toured the country. In 1943, George became the first African American to play with Stan Kenton. George played with Kenton until 1945, leaving to play with Count Basie and others until he retired to St. Louis in 1949.[71]

St. Louisan Forrest Crawford was known to have worked with the Joe Gillis band in 1934. He soon moved to New York and recorded with Dick Robertson, Red McKenzie, the Mound City Blowers, Harry Richman and Bunny Berigan.[72] Crawford contracted tuberculosis in 1937 and returned to St. Louis. He led a band at the Showboat Ballroom in 1939.[73]

Alto saxophonist Tab Smith was born in North Carolina and played with many national big bands and led his own groups. He was in and out of St. Louis from 1933 until he came back permanently in the early 1960s. Smith died in 1971 after teaching music and working in real estate.[74]

Gordon Jenkins was born in Webster Groves. He was an arranger and composer with a career in radio, theater and film. He worked in a band in

Floyd Smith (*top*) and Dick Wilson. *Photographer, William P. Gottlieb. William P. Gottlieb Collection, Library of Congress, Washington, D.C. Public domain.*

Jimmy Blanton, early 1940s. *Courtesy Alamy Stock Photos, Vectors and Videos, New York.*

Steelville, Missouri (1926–29), and then worked for Isham Jones. He is best known for composing Benny Goodman's theme song, "Goodbye."[75]

Other well-known musicians who were born in St. Louis but never worked here are the Buckner brothers—saxophonist Ted and pianist Milt Buckner—and vocalist Billy Banks, born in Alton. Their careers are not covered here.

Another technological shift occurred in the late 1930s. By 1939, wooden riverboats were being phased out because of safety regulations. They tended to burn to the waterline if a fire started. By 1940, all of these boats were replaced by the *President* and the *Admiral*, both constructed of steel. Marable and Jackson played their last riverboat jobs in 1940 and 1941.

We close this chapter with the discovery of bassist Jimmy Blanton. Blanton was born in Chattanooga, Tennessee, in 1918. He came to St. Louis in 1939 during his summer vacation, astounding everyone. Hayes Pillars offered him a job and bought him a full-sized bass. Blanton had short gigs with Eddie Randle and other St. Louis bands. Duke Ellington was working at the Coronado Hotel from October 10 to November 2, 1939. Sometime during this engagement, Blanton was playing in a jam session at Jesse Johnson's Deluxe Café about six blocks away. It was there that Ellington discovered him and hired him. There are six different versions of Blanton's discovery recounted in *City of Gabriels: The Jazz History of St. Louis 1895–1973.*[76] What really happened is not fully known. What we do know is that a broadcast of the Ellington band with Blanton on bass was recorded on November 1, 1939.[77]

Blanton revolutionized bass playing but died too young, in Los Angeles, from tuberculosis in 1942. Milt Hinton described trying to bring comfort to Blanton during his last days in a sanatorium by visiting him and dedicating songs to him on Cab Calloway's Los Angeles radio broadcasts [*Hinton Interview*].

The year 1939 also brought fears of the coming war in Europe. How St. Louis and its jazz musicians survived it is detailed in chapter 4.

Chapter 4

WORLD WAR II AND ITS AFTERMATH

As the clouds of war were building in Europe in the late 1930s, the need for live entertainment continued in St. Louis. The *Post-Dispatch* and the *Argus* noted that all of the touring big bands made stops in St. Louis at quite a number of venues: Forest Park Highlands, Sauter's Park and Pavilion, the Chase Hotel, the Westminster and Imperial Ballrooms (all on Kingshighway), the Fox Theater and the Grand Central Theater (both on Grand), the Coronado Hotel (on Market west of Grand), the Lynn Theater (Grandel Square), the Castle Ballroom (Twenty-Ninth and Olive), the Arcadia Ballroom (soon to become Tunetown), the Showboat and the Casa Loma Ballrooms. Local bands often played in these halls. The Jeter-Pillars Band worked at Tunetown and the Fox Theater, Dewey Jackson at the Castle Ballroom and Sauter's Park and Russ David at the Casa Loma. Will Osborne and Del Courtney led the house bands at Tunetown. At the West End Waiters Club, located at Vandeventer and Enright, John "Buggs" Roberts led the band into the early 1950s.

Club Plantation moved from the Vandeventer building to one that housed the Palladium Club on Delmar just north of the Fox Theater. The Jeter-Pillars Orchestra continued as the house band at the club until 1944. The Plantation brought in other bands. Louis Armstrong, the Mills Brothers, the George Hudson Orchestra, Earl Hines, Andy Kirk, Noble Sissle, Ella Fitzgerald and Billy Eckstine were noted in newspaper ads. After the war ended, any establishment with entertainment began to struggle because of the 1947 entertainment tax.[78] The *Post-Dispatch* of June 5, 1948, reported that the Plantation closed for good.

Club Riviera opened in June 1944. Politician Jordan Chambers opened it as an African American alternative to Club Plantation. In its heyday, Club Riviera had many ads in black and white newspapers. It presented Billy Eckstine, Lucky Millinder, Benny Carter, Earl Hines, Tiny Bradshaw, Eddie "Cleanhead" Vinson, the International Sweethearts of Rhythm, Woody Herman, Georgie Auld and local bands. *Post-Dispatch* data show that the Riviera was open only sporadically after June 1947. The Riviera was unusual for a venue in St. Louis in the 1940s, as it had an integrated clientele. The phrase "everybody welcome" was seen on many of the Riviera's ads. The bandstand was integrated in a jam session that happened on October 18, 1945, with personnel from the Cootie Williams, Lionel Hampton and Jack Teagarden bands. Charlie Menees reviewed the proceedings in the *Post-Dispatch*.

Lloyd Smith (1914–1999), a highly trained multi-instrumentalist, worked with many local and national bands and recorded with Earl Hines from 1944 to 1946. He returned to St. Louis and opened the Musicians Club, an after-hours establishment, in 1947. According to Smith, just about every celebrity who came to St. Louis until 1955 visited his club. He mentored many young musicians and was the father of the Bosman twins (see chapters 8–10).[79]

After 1943, the *Post-Dispatch* noted that Kiel Auditorium and Opera House also brought in many national bands and, later in the decade, package shows like Jazz at the Philharmonic. The 1943 Christmas night double bill at Kiel featured George Hudson's and Duke Ellington's bands. On the next night, the Louis Armstrong Orchestra and the white Johnny Lyons band had a band battle. A 1945 performance at Kiel Auditorium featuring Ellington was advertised as the first "real" jazz concert in St. Louis, because no dancing was allowed. Charlie Menees reviewed the sold-out March 13, 1949 Jazz at the Philharmonic concert.

The *Post-Dispatch* and *Argus* noted a number of small venues where jazz was heard. Fate Marable worked at Club 93 Gardens on Natural Bridge in 1941 and 1942 and also at the Victoria Club. The Circus Snack Bar at the Forest Park Hotel began having both local and national musicians in 1944. In 1945, the Tommy Dean band was at the Rainbow Room in Alton, Illinois. He then had a long-running job at the Forest Park Hotel. Accordionist Joe Mooney played there in 1947. Tenor saxophonist Jimmy Forrest recorded at a small downtown club in 1946 [*Discography*]. Other establishments were the Palace Gardens (on Finney), the Blue Flame Club in East St. Louis, Club Bolo (on Easton), Club 211 (on Cardinal), the Cozy Corner Tavern and the Stage Bar (on Cass).

The Glass Bar was located in the Midtown Hotel on Lawton (where St. Louis University's athletic fields are now found). It opened in 1944, and during the rest of the decade, Tommy Dean and local rhythm and blues bands were popular acts, until 1950, when the club started bringing in national acts. In an ad in the November 28, 1948 edition of the *Argus*, drummer Ben Thigpen had a group called his "Interracial Combo" in the Glass Bar. The ad for the group identified who was white and who was black.

During World War II, a number of jazz musicians served in the military along with the general population. Some of the army veterans were Harold "Shorty" Baker, James Boyd Jr., Sammy Gardner, George Votaw, Vertna Saunders, Bruz Woods, Foots Goodson, Wendell Marshall, Theodore Bibb and Ralph Sutton. According to the May 3, 1945 edition of the *Post-Dispatch*, Wendell Marshall was wounded in Germany in the previous month. U.S. Army Air Force veterans included Charles Fox and Muggsy Sprecher. Quite a few were navy veterans: Clark Terry, Ernie Wilkins, Jimmy Wilkins, Charles Pillars, Sykes Smith, Cliff and Ed Batchman, Len Bowden, Arvell Shaw, Leroy Harris Jr., Jim Bohlen, Jimmy Kennedy, Dudley Brooks, Richard Haley, Raymond Eldridge Sr., Arvelle Shaw and Robert Carter.

None of the branches of the military was integrated when the war started, a situation that remained until President Harry Truman desegregated them in 1948. Interestingly, Eleanor Roosevelt, wife of former president Franklin Roosevelt, recommended that blacks in the navy should have other jobs than just stewards.[80] According to Clark Terry, St. Louis bandleader Len Bowden recruited a lot of black musicians out of St. Louis [*Terry Interview*]. Ernie Wilkins recalled that the navy recruited musicians to play in service bands. The training base for many black and white navy musicians was the Great Lakes Naval Training Center north of Chicago. Many nationally known musicians trained at Great Lakes and were then shipped out to various bands.

Some musicians, as with the general populace, did not serve in the military for various reasons. With few exceptions, St. Louis jazz musicians always have worked day jobs to support their families. During and after the war, Singleton Palmer worked at Scullin Steel and played in its marching band. According to Palmer, nearly all of George Hudson's band members played in this forty- to fifty-piece band, which was directed by William Rollins [*Palmer Interview*]. Eddie Randle worked in a munitions plant.

The Jeter-Pillars Orchestra remained the house band of the Plantation until 1944. In 1942, the band won a contest outright to play on the *Fitch Bandwagon* show, but they were forced to share the broadcast with a white band to be allowed on the air. Louis Armstrong's manager, Joe Glaser, also offered the band a job, but "Big Tony" Scarpelli and his "friends" would not let the band go.[81] The orchestra opened Club Riviera in June 1944. In January 1945, they went on the road to Chicago and then traveled as part of a package show with Louis Jordan that traveled to New York, Washington, D.C., Detroit and Chicago.[82] They returned to the Plantation and worked from May to September, when they left again to tour with the "Red Hot and Blues" USO tour to New England for three months and then to the Philippines and Japan for six months. St. Louis musicians Walter "Crack" Stanley (trumpet), Hayes Pillars, Charles Pillars, James Jeter (reeds) and John Cotter (piano) were on the tour. Returning to St. Louis, the Jeter-Pillars Orchestra was reorganized with all St. Louis musicians for an engagement at Club Riviera. Then they played two more engagements at the Apollo in New York in late 1946 and mid-1947.[83]

Eddie Johnson, the riverboat bandleader in the 1930s, continued to lead bands in St. Louis in the 1940s. His band played the last engagement before the Plantation closed. Johnson, always the entrepreneur, moved to New York and opened his own booking agency to book his band. While in New York, he took theory classes at New York University and worked in a hospital for

Jeter-Pillars Orchestra and USO Review, circa 1946. *Courtesy of the E. Azalia Hackley Collection of African Americans in the Performing Arts, Detroit Public Library.*

the six-month waiting period required by the New York musicians' union. Johnson returned to St. Louis in 1950 [*Johnson Interview*]. His further exploits will be covered in chapter 5.

Alabama Jazz Hall of Fame inductee George Hudson (1910–1996) was born in Stonewall, Mississippi, and lived his childhood in Birmingham, Alabama. He took music lessons early and settled on trumpet. His family moved to Pittsburgh. Hudson was with Zack White when he joined Alphonso Trent in 1930. The formation of the Jeter-Pillars Orchestra out of the Trent band was recounted in chapter 3. Hudson left Trent and made his way to Kansas City and worked with the Oklahoma Blue Devils and Bennie Moten. The Jeter-Pillars Orchestra recruited him in 1934 to be their lead trumpet player. Four years later, Hudson left the Jeter-Pillars Orchestra to work with Dewey Jackson. Hudson's band made its debut at the 1942 "Y" Circus [*Hudson Interview*].

The *Post-Dispatch* noted Hudson's band working all over St. Louis, including jobs at the "Y" Circus for several years [*Hudson Interview*]. They went into the Plantation in 1944, replacing the Jeter-Pillars Orchestra. This was during the war, when musicians were hard to find.

The "Y" Circus was an annual show that ran from 1935 to 1955 at Kiel Auditorium. It was an entertainment-fundraiser for the Pine Street YMCA. Some of these presentations ran for six days, with acts that included both local and national jazz musicians. Cab Calloway (1944) and Count Basie (1945) headlined two of the events.

After the war, Clark Terry, Ernie Wilkins and others joined the Hudson band. They toured the Midwest and then went east to New York and played the Apollo Theater and the Savoy Ballroom. At the Apollo, they played opposite the Illinois Jacquet Band. Jacquet had a big hit with "Body and Soul." When Hudson's band played their arrangement of "Body and Soul," with "Weasel" Parker taking the solo, the audience reaction was so strong that the Apollo management insisted George take the number out of his part of the show so as not to compete with Jacquet's version. Hudson told the Apollo management that he would only take "Body and Soul" out when he took the band out of the theater, and he did [*Hudson Interview*]. The band remained on the road until 1950, playing theaters and backing Louis Jordan, Ella Fitzgerald and others. An interesting sidelight to the sojourn of this band is that pianist Fritz Jones played his first road job with the band in 1949. He was later known as Ahmad Jamal [*Jamal Interview*].

Hudson's band recorded four titles for King Records in Cincinnati in 1949 [*Discography*]. One problem that Hudson had with his band was that

Clark Terry (*left*) and George Hudson. *Roscoe Crenshaw, photographer. Used with permission of Gwen Terry.*

he was always using arrangements from other famous bands and had no identifiable style. Hudson came off the road in 1950 and started teaching at Lovejoy High School in Brooklyn, Illinois. George kept his band going until the late 1980s, playing one-nighters in and close to St. Louis. Many of these musicians were local music teachers [*Hudson Interview*].

Ernie Wilkins was George Hudson's chief arranger. He was born in 1922 into a family that loved music. After taking violin lessons from age ten, Ernie learned saxophone from Jimmy Forrest. Wilkins was fascinated by the arrangements of the big bands and became a professional musician when he graduated from high school. Ernie joined the Blue Devils in 1938 and was encouraged by Randle to write for the band [*Wilkins Interview*]. Wilkins went to Wilberforce University and joined the navy as a musician in 1942. He was at the Great Lakes Naval Station, playing with Clark Terry and other well-known musicians. Returning to St. Louis after the war, Wilkins worked around the city. He worked with Earl Hines in 1947 and then returned to St. Louis to play with Hudson. Wilkins wrote "Applejack Boogie," the band's theme. He remained with Hudson until the band stopped touring [*Wilkins Interview*]. Ernie's further adventures in St. Louis will be recounted in chapter 5.

On May Day in 1941, Clark Terry was in Carbondale, Illinois, playing in a park with Benny Reed for an interscholastic event. High school bands were also playing. The East St. Louis Lincoln band, led by Elwood Buchanan, was one of those bands. A very timid teenager wanted some advice on trumpet playing and approached Terry, who fluffed him off because he was more interested in the girls around the bandstand. That trumpeter was fifteen-year-old Miles Davis. The next time Terry saw Miles, he was playing with Eddie Randle's Blue Devils at the St. Louis Elks Club in 1942 [*Terry Interview*]. Clark and Miles were close friends until Miles died in 1991.

Eddie Randle's St. Louis Blue Devils returned to St. Louis in 1941 from a residency in Sodus Point, New York, and began a permanent stay in St. Louis. He was at the Club 400, the Castle Ballroom, the Club Rhumboogie, the Cozy Corner and the Elks Club. In September 1941, the band was recorded noncommercially at a St. Louis club [*Discography*]. The recordings show that the Blue Devils played a variety of music. When he went into a club, Randle would check what was on the club jukebox and tailor the band's presentation to that [*Randle Interview*].

Early in 1942, Randle hired sixteen-year-old Miles Davis. Apparently, Miles and another well-schooled trumpeter were competing for the position. Randle took Miles because he thought that he showed a lot of promise and was going to go far [*Randle Interview*]. Eddie had a gift for reading people and knowing what they needed from him. Because of the war, he began to wind down his career in music by 1943 and to pay more attention to his funeral business. Randle did continue to lead bands until 1963.

Miles Davis (1926–1991) may be the most significant musician ever to play in jazz. Most musicians never change the course of music history. Some do so one time, but Miles changed the course of twentieth-century music four times. He was born in Alton, Illinois. His father was a prominent oral surgeon. The family moved to East St. Louis. Elwood Buchanan was Miles's trumpet teacher from his junior high years through high school at East St. Louis Lincoln High School.[84] Buchanan told all of his students to play straight tones without a heavy vibrato because they would begin to shake when they got older [*Buchanan Interview*]. Miles also studied with Joseph Gustat, who recommended the Heim mouthpiece that Miles used for the rest of his career.

Buchanan was the one who recommended Miles to Eddie Randle. Miles soon became the Blue Devils' music director. Miles also played with the "Duke" Brooks group and became friends with another trumpeter, Bobby Danzig,[85] who was in the Blue Devils with him for a short time. Miles and

Danzig would practice all day and then call each other on the telephone and play things they learned. At night, when they were not working, they would visit various clubs to soak up musical knowledge. Miles would visit the "Buggs" Roberts band at the West End Waiters Club and look over trumpeter Vertna Saunders's shoulder. Everything the Roberts band played was written out, and Miles waited for Saunders to make a mistake; it never happened. Miles also apparently liked Levi Madison's trumpet sound.

Miles stayed with Randle until 1944. During this time, well-known musicians noticed Miles's work with Randle. He began to get offers from several nationally known big bands, but Miles's mother would not let him go.[86] On July 7, 1944, the Billy Eckstine band began a three-week engagement at the Plantation. This was the most musically advanced band in jazz at the time, with Dizzy Gillespie, Charlie Parker, Sarah Vaughan and other modernists.

The management of the Plantation was not pleased with the band. Nine days later, they were at Club Riviera, switching venues with the Jeter-Pillars band. Two members of the band, Dizzy Gillespie and Art Blakey, said that it was because the band had crossed a number of racial lines.[87] But Hayes Pillars said that it was because the band would not compromise and play music to please the customers.[88] No one really knows what happened. The *Argus*, *Globe-Democrat* and *Post-Dispatch* all carried ads related to the switch, but nothing else was reported. All we have are the conflicting reports of the three musicians. Perhaps "Big Tony" and his friends put the word out for the papers to remain silent.

During the Eckstine engagement at the Riviera, Miles Davis was asked to substitute for trumpeter Buddy Anderson, who became ill. Miles said he couldn't read the charts because he was listening to Gillespie and Parker.[89] Years later, Billy Eckstine said that Miles "sounded terrible, he couldn't play at all."[90] Bobby Danzig said that both the St. Louis musicians and the musicians in the Eckstine band laughed at him. This experience would have crushed most people, but Miles's determination, which so impressed Eddie Randle, carried him to the Juilliard School of Music in New York and onto the national scene.

In the fall of 1944, Miles went to New York and passed his Juilliard audition. Eventually, Charlie Parker started rooming with him. Miles began working with Parker in mid-1945 and never returned to Juilliard. He played with Parker until 1948, making many recordings. By 1949, he was leading bands that changed the course of twentieth-century music four times.[91] A discussion of these movements in jazz is beyond the scope of this book.

Charlie Parker (*left*) and Miles Davis, 1947. *Photographer William P. Gottlieb. William P. Gottlieb Collection, Library of Congress, Washington D.C. Public domain.*

Never in good health, Miles died from a combination of a stroke, pneumonia and respiratory failure.

Clark Terry's story continues with him and Ernie Wilkins joining the navy at the Great Lakes Naval Training Center. Clark was not shipped out to serve at other bases but stayed in Chicago the entire time. St. Louisan Len Bowden led the band and staffed it with a lot of his friends. Clark was able to visit the Chicago clubs to keep his technique sharp [*Terry Interview*].

Returning to St. Louis after being mustered out, Terry began playing with the George Hudson band and soon was the "straw boss." Clark then joined the Charlie Barnet band for a year in 1947. During his stay with Barnet, he recorded six sides for V-Disc; three were issued. The group was called "Clark Terry and His Section Eights," a reference to the military term for personnel having mental problems. Clark also recorded with Eddie "Cleanhead" Vinson in St. Louis the same year [*both in Discography*]. Clark and "Weasel"

Parker joined Count Basie in 1948 and stayed through the breakup of the band in 1950, playing with Basie's sextet and septet. He recruited Singleton Palmer in 1948 and helped put Basie's new band together in 1951. Clark Terry's stays with Duke Ellington, the *Tonight Show* orchestra, his teaching and his freelance work are beyond the scope of the book. He was the subject of an endearing documentary, *Keep on Keeping On*, before his death on February 21, 2015. Terry was a beloved figure in jazz.

Pianist Ralph Sutton (1922–2001) was born in Hamburg, Missouri, a town in St. Charles County that no longer exists. He and his sister Barbara became jazz pianists. Ralph began piano at age nine. Like Miles Davis, he listened to *Harlem Rhythm* on WIL and was taken with the stride piano of Fats Waller. He dedicated his life to preserving that tradition. Ralph was at Northeast Missouri State College when he left to join Jack Teagarden in 1942. Sutton was drafted in 1943 and served in the army until 1945.[92] Returning to St. Louis, Sutton worked for two years in various clubs until 1947, when he left for New York. In the 1950s and '60s, he was a regular visitor to St. Louis. Sutton worked all over the world for the rest of his life and is the subject of a biography, *Piano Man*, by James Schacter. Gaslight Records recorded him twice and once with his sister in St. Louis during the later years of his life [*Discography*]. Ralph died in Colorado in 2001.

Ralph Sutton, 1987.
Photograph by Dennis Owsley.

Born in St. Louis to a female bandleader, tenor saxophonist Jimmy Forrest (1920–1980) worked with just about everybody until he left with the Don Albert Band.[93] Jay McShann then beckoned (1940–42). Forrest then was with Andy Kirk until 1948 and worked with Duke Ellington that same year. In between jobs, Forrest was in and out of St. Louis from 1946 to 1950, playing at various clubs, including the Glass Bar.[94] Forrest recorded with pianist Charles Fox at a club in St. Louis for the Town label in 1946 [*Discography*]. See chapter 5 for more on Jimmy Forrest.

Bassist Wendell Marshall (1920–2002) was Jimmy Blanton's cousin. He went to Lincoln University, played with Lionel Hampton and was in the army (1943–46). After the war, Wendell worked with many groups and led his own trio in St. Louis.[95] His first recordings were made with the Stuff Smith Quartet in 1946 for the Town and Country label [*Discography*]. In 1947, Marshall joined Mercer Ellington and, four months later, the Duke himself. He left Ellington in 1955 and worked as a New York studio musician until he retired to St. Louis in 1968.

The Town and Country label also recorded Tommy Dean and His St. Louisans in late 1947 [*Discography*]. This date is the first for saxophonist Chris Woods. Both recorded together in Chicago in 1950. See chapter 5 for more on these musicians.

Vocalist Velma Middleton (1917–1961) began her career in local clubs and then joined Louis Armstrong,[96] where she stayed until the end of her life.[97] Armstrong married his wife, Lucille, in October 1942 in Middleton's backyard. Bassist Arvell Shaw (1923–1992) played with Fate Marable in 1942 and then joined the navy. He then worked with Louis Armstrong's big bands and small group and other jazz greats until his death.[98]

The decade of the 1940s ended with the repression of the "Red Scare" that became McCarthyism. The clouds of war were once again on the horizon.

Chapter 5

THE EXPANSION OF JAZZ IN ST. LOUIS

The early 1950s was a time of expansion for jazz venues and performances in St. Louis. More clubs than ever were presenting jazz on both sides of the river [*Mixon Interview*]. A scene developed in an area known as the DeBaliviere Strip, on DeBaliviere going south from the intersection with Delmar. The Glass Bar was very prominent at this time. But Club Riviera finally gave up the ghost in late 1950. Most bandstands and clubs were still segregated. Dixieland jazz was gaining momentum in St. Louis, leading to more work for the older musicians.

The *Post-Dispatch* listed ads for many national jazz groups at Kiel Auditorium and Opera House. Often these concerts were packages of two or more artists, such as Jazz at the Philharmonic (1951, 1952 and 1956). Other concerts featured Louis Armstrong and Benny Goodman (1953), Art Blakey, Herbie Mann, Chris Connor and Chet Baker (1957), "Jazz for Moderns" (1957) and one with Ahmad Jamal, Dakota Staton and Shelly Manne (1959).

Jimmy Forrest returned to St. Louis in 1950. He was working in clubs and as a clerk in the records department of the Gamen Appliance Company [*Menees Interview*]. He began recording for a label in Chicago called United and, in 1951, recorded "Night Train," a hit record with both the general public and strippers [*Discography*], using St. Louis musicians as sidemen. "Night Train" is an almost note-for-note theft of the opening riff from Ellington's "Happy Go Lucky Local." Forrest and Miles Davis were also heard on a bootleg recording at the Barrel in 1952 [*Discography*]. The tunes were standard performance fare for the time. After working around St.

Club Riviera, 1947. *Courtesy of the Mercantile Library at the University of Missouri–St. Louis.*

Louis, Forrest went to New York. His subsequent career is beyond the scope of this book.[99]

In 1951, Ernie Wilkins and his brother got a telephone call from Clark Terry, who recruited musicians for Count Basie. In the 1940s, he had recruited Singleton Palmer and "Weasel" Parker and, in 1950, Bob Graf for the Basie Septet [*Terry Interview*]. Graf then spent time with Woody Herman. Basie needed an alto player, but Ernie played tenor, so he borrowed an alto from a member of his mother's church [*Wilkins Interview*]. The brothers got on the train to New York. Terry also told Basie of Ernie's arranging and composing skills. This eventually led to the famous 1954 arrangement of "Every Day I Have the Blues" featuring Joe Williams on vocal. Ernie wrote the arrangement in one afternoon, and it was used in that night's performance.

Ernie's arranging and composing career was very fruitful. He left Basie in 1955 to freelance. This was during the drug epidemic of the late 1940s to mid-1950s; sadly, Wilkins developed a heroin addiction. In order to

Ernie Wilkins. *Courtesy Don and Heidi Wolff Jazz Institute, Harris Stowe State University, St. Louis.*

rescue his friend, Clark Terry formed a quintet with him. Wilkins was the chief arranger for Clark's Big B-A-D Band in 1968. After a tour of Europe with Terry, Ernie settled in Copenhagen, Denmark, where he worked until his death in 1999.[100] His brother Jimmy Wilkins had a long and active career leading big bands in Detroit and Las Vegas and died at age ninety-five in 2018.[101]

Pianist Tommy Dean (1909–1965) was born in Louisiana and worked with the St. Louis Blue Devils in 1941. After leaving Randle, he started his own group, touring the Midwest. Dean reached Chicago in 1945 and moved between there and St. Louis throughout the rest of his life. Working at the Glass Bar and other clubs in St. Louis, Dean brought saxophonist Chris Woods into his group [*Discography*]. As the 1950s wore on, Dean turned more and more to rhythm and blues. He died suddenly in 1965.[102]

Saxophonist Chris Woods (1925–1985) was born in Memphis and moved to St. Louis shortly after World War II ended. He worked with Jeter-Pillars, George Hudson and Tommy Dean. Woods then worked around St. Louis and recorded for the United label [*Discography*]. He recorded a tune called "Somebody Done Stole My Blues" in 1953 (not released until 1973). Sonny Stitt stole it from a Woods performance and recorded it as "Loose Walk."

To make ends meet, Woods worked at teenage dances in South St. Louis, playing the rock 'n' roll hits. He quit music and became a bus driver for nine months.[103] In 1955, Woods again worked as a musician but also on his day job. He left St. Louis in 1961 and toured the world. Chris Woods died of cancer in 1985. A moving tribute to him can be found in the *Terry Interview*.

Oliver Nelson (1932–1975) was a reed player/composer-arranger born in St. Louis who worked around town in the late 1940s and then left St. Louis for a larger career. He ended up in the military during the Korean War, playing in bands (1952–54). He then returned to St. Louis, studying composition and theory at Washington University (1954–57) and Lincoln University in Columbia, Missouri (1957–58) and then left for New York.[104] Chapter 6 will present his 1960s contributions to St. Louis jazz.

Eddie Johnson returned from New York and began working in venues on both sides of the river, often in the company of Tab Smith. He worked for eleven years with Leroy Harris Jr. at the King Brothers Motel (now the Breckenridge). Johnson also had a label, ELJ Records, that recorded everything, including two sides with vocalist Joe Buckner and two sides with Smith [*Johnson Interview*].

Drummer Elijah "Lyge" Shaw (1900–1982) was born in Jackson, Tennessee. He had extensive experience playing all sorts of percussion instruments, a product of his time playing in minstrel shows, vaudeville acts, circuses and carnivals. He was in and out of St. Louis from 1917 on and was instrumental in getting the black musicians' union reinstated in 1944. He played on the riverboats and with Eddie Johnson at the Showboat. He decided to get out of performing and into piano tuning and became one of the top piano tuners in St. Louis.[105] His chance discussion with Mary Ruth in University City set something in motion that was to not only enhance St. Louis jazz but also divide the audience into two groups that increasingly had little contact with each other.

Ms. Ruth asked him if he knew the older musicians and how to contact them. She apparently thought that if someone could get them together, they might be able to revive the riverboat music. Shaw was president of the black musicians' union and gave her the names. She followed up and invited them to a jam session–party at her house. She couldn't pay them, but she supplied the food and drink. The parties happened once a month and lasted until 2:00 or 3:00 a.m.

One of the owners of the Barrel on the DeBaliviere Strip came to one of the parties. That led to Dixieland jam sessions at the Barrel on Saturdays and, finally, a nightly gig. The bandstand was integrated in these sessions, but the Barrel had to stop the nightly gigs because it was losing money. Jam sessions then started at the Universal Dance Studios on Delmar [*Palmer Interview*]. The crowds got too large there, and the show moved to a barge anchored on the river called the *Fort Gay*. The police used the pretext of a drunken customer to shut down the jam sessions, even though alcohol was not sold at the venue.[106]

One of the great tuba players in all of music, Singleton Palmer (1912–1993), was born in St. Louis. He was taken by music at an early age, took piano lessons and was playing cornet by age eleven. Palmer joined the Mose Wiley Band at age fourteen, but during hard times in 1928 he was going to be let go when his stepfather bought him a tuba. He played with the Oliver Cobb Rhythm Kings and Crackerjacks until 1932. After switching to string bass, he played with Dewey Jackson (1934–41). During the war, Palmer played with George Hudson and Jimmy Forrest while working at Scullin Steel. He also played in its band. Clark Terry got Singleton into the Basie band in 1947, a job that lasted to 1950. That year, he started his Dixieland Six and was active in the jam sessions chronicled above [*Palmer Interview*].

Palmer's first band was racially mixed—three blacks and three whites. Barbara Sutton, Ralph's sister, played piano. The Snack Bar at the Forest Park Hotel was interested in Palmer's band, but it couldn't hire them

Singleton Palmer, 1980. *Photograph by Dennis Owsley.*

Leroy Harris, 1980. *Photograph by Dennis Owsley.*

until they replaced the whites [*Palmer Interview*]. The band stayed at the Snack Bar for eight months. It made a 1950 recording for the Disco label with two issued sides [*Discography*]. Musicians in Palmer's groups over the years included trumpeters Dewey Jackson, Benny Starks and Andrew Webb Jr.; trombonists Leon King and Robert Carter; clarinetists Al Guichard and Norman Mason; clarinetist–alto saxophonist Leroy Harris Jr.; pianists Gus Perryman and Robert "Bunky" Parker; and drummers "Lyge" Shaw, Ben Thigpen and Rick O'Connor. Palmer was a major star during the Gaslight Square period (see chapter 6 for the rest of Palmer's career).

Before discussing the St. Louis Jazz Club, we will detour into a discussion of the differences between "traditional" jazz and Dixieland.[107] Many Dixieland fans believe they are hearing the music played just like "Jelly Roll" Morton did. In traditional jazz (1900–25), tubas were not used in small combos; the first use of a tuba in a small combo was in the 1927 Louis Armstrong Hot Seven and was uncommon until 1939. String basses were used in small combos. Until then, tubas were always used in large ensembles. If we believe the photographs of early jazz groups, the front-line instruments were trumpet, trombone, clarinet and violin in various combinations of three. Dixieland combos have trumpet, trombone and clarinet front lines. The drums usually had one cymbal, a bass drum and a snare drum. Dixieland combos use a full drum kit, with the style closer to bebop drumming. Present-day Dixieland arose around the same time as bebop as a conservative alternate to an increasingly moribund swing style (1939–40). Bebop was the progressive alternate. When Dixieland was first played, its repertoire came exclusively from the white Original Dixieland Jazz Band and the white New Orleans Rhythm Kings.

The St. Louis Jazz Club has been in active existence since 1951. Bob and Vivian Ostwald, Charlie Menees, Mary Ruth, Singleton Palmer (Mary's husband), "Lyge" Shaw, Barbara Curtis, Skip Diringer and others started it about a month after the Singleton Palmer recordings [*Menees and Leopold Interviews*]. After a slow start, the club began producing concerts that featured racially mixed bands. An annual cruise called "Jazz on the River" on the *Admiral* lasted for seven years. The Jazz Club held a jazz Mass at St. Bridget's Catholic Church for seven years and had a joint concert with the symphony and jazz vespers at Christ Church Cathedral. The *Post-Dispatch* of the early to mid-1950s had several articles and letters to the editor questioning the place of jazz in a church. Among them were an anti-jazz article by Thomas B. Sherman (September 1, 1957), an article by Rufus Terrell attempting to define jazz that left out everything but Dixieland (August 27, 1954) and a July 3, 1955 article on the Jazz Club that stated their members' dislike of bebop. At its most popular, the club had a hand in three hundred gigs per year for Dixieland musicians [*Leopold Interview*]. It cosponsored the first St. Louis Jazz Festival at Kiel Auditorium on July 7, 1958. The headliners were an all-star Dixieland group led by Singleton Palmer and a modern group led by pianist John Cotter featuring St. Louis favorite Hugh "Peanuts" Whalum. It continues to meet with monthly concerts. Their activities in St. Louis jazz will be detailed in subsequent chapters. It can be stated that their focus has changed from racially integrated Dixieland and 1930s swing styles to exclusively Dixieland.

In 1950, Bob Koester was a record collector taking business courses at St. Louis University while at the same time reselling records he had bought from secondhand stores out of his dorm room. He became a charter member of the Jazz Club. Both Clark Terry and Bob Graf were at the founding meeting. Koester also met a man named Ron Fister who collected mainly pop music. They started a business that eventually became the Blue Note Record Shop. By this time, he and Fister had split up, and Koester moved to a location on Delmar near the DeBaliviere Strip. He started a label called Delmar Records and began making records by the time he was twenty-one. His first recording was an LP with Sammy Gardner in July 1953. Gardner also recorded three LPs on Mound City Records around this time. Koester recorded the Dixie Stompers in 1953 and 1954 and made more recordings in 1956 [*All Discography*]. In 1958, he moved to Chicago and founded an institution in that city, the Jazz Record Mart. He changed the label's name to Delmark. Koester has another label, Nessa, that presents music by Chicago's avant-garde musicians.[108] Bob Koester is still selling music in Chicago.

The opening paragraph of this chapter mentioned the DeBaliviere Strip, the place that may have been the first major jazz scene in St. Louis. Incidentally, the DeBaliviere Strip lasted longer than the more famous

Gaslight Square. Clubs and musicians started cropping up there in the late 1940s. In 1948, the *Post-Dispatch* mentioned two engagements: Jimmy Forrest and Ralph Sutton. In 1952, Forrest was recorded with Miles Davis at the Barrel. The next week, Dewey Jackson was recorded with pianist Don Ewell [*Discography*], showing the eclecticism of the time. In addition to the Barrel, clubs in this area were the Windermere Bar (drummer Joe Smith's Riverboat Ramblers with Sammy Gardner, 1951), Sorrento's (a popular spot for jam sessions), the Top Hat, the Spa, Charlie Wells's Tiger's Den and Little Nero's. The Mound City Jazz Band, Rick O'Connor's Saints and the Dixie Stompers were heard on the Strip. Trombonist Norman Menne was jamming in the area at age thirteen and never had problems [*Menne Interview*]. He described it as good, clean fun.

Pianist Herb Drury was working at French Village in East St. Louis in 1954 when Jerry Cherry subbed for his regular bass player. This was the beginning of a partnership that lasted until Cherry's death in 2000. They have performed as a trio with drummers Phil Hulsey and Art Heagle. They had a trio or a quartet when TV personality Jim Bohlen occasionally played with them. They played for many years at Sorrento's on DeBaliviere. Drury also was the pianist in the Jazz Central group. In addition to performing, Herb taught classical and jazz piano at the St. Louis Conservatory and at the University of Missouri–St. Louis for twenty-two years. Throughout his career, he also taught privately. Most of the major pianists in St. Louis have taken lessons from him. He retired around 2014. For a video portrait of Herb, visit YouTube.[109]

Herb Drury (*left*) and Jerry Cherry, 2000. *Photograph by Dennis Owsley with permissions from Herb Drury and Tim Cherry.*

The Glass Bar's history goes back to 1944. Located in the Midtown Hotel at Compton and Lawton, now under the St. Louis University athletic field, the Glass Bar featured local rhythm and blues groups alternating with jazz groups. In 1955, it was refurbished and renamed Peacock Alley. As time went on, the Glass Bar became the scene for modern jazz, bringing in nationally known musicians. This policy started on May 18, 1951, with Stan Getz, a very popular attraction, headlining at the venue. He returned twice more in 1951. The *Post-Dispatch* and *Argus* listed engagements at the venue by James Moody, Dizzy Gillespie, Gene Ammons, Sonny Stitt, Lester Young, Charlie Parker, Bud Powell and Art Blakey's Jazz Messengers. Firsthand stories by Walter Dixon, the bouncer at the club, include both Charlie Parker and Bud Powell [*Dixon Interview*].

The first great Miles Davis quintet visited the Glass Bar on two occasions, in October 1955 and July 1956. Jesse "Spider" Burks, the emcee and a St. Louis jazz radio personality, taped the band on July 14 and July 21. Eventually, a CD called *Spider Burks and the Miles Davis Quintet at Peacock Alley* was released on the Soulard label in 1956 [*Discography*]. The tunes were from the quintet's working repertoire.

Bernie Thrasher, a semiprofessional photographer and jazz fan, photographed some of the 1955–59 Peacock Alley engagements.[110] There are photographic records of the Davis quintet, Chet Baker, Max Roach, Chico Hamilton, J.J. Johnson, Art Blakey, Carmen McRae and Sonny Stitt. Local tenor saxophonist Bob Graf was photographed and recorded by Delmar Records in February 1958 [*Discography*]. Graf, with tenor saxophonist Ron Ruff, also recorded on January 27, 1958, at Westminster College in Fulton, Missouri.

Bob Graf (1927–1981) was born in St. Louis. His friend Clark Terry got him a job with a Count Basie small group in 1950, but Wardell Gray soon replaced him. Graf then connected with Woody Herman, recording with him in 1950 and 1951.[111] Graf's sojourns in Los Angeles and with Gerry Mulligan are beyond the scope of this book. He returned to St. Louis in 1958 and was recorded with vocalist Bev Kelly on VGM Records in 1959 [*Discography*]. In late 1959, Graf worked with guitarist Grant Green, organist Sam Lazar and Chauncey Williams. Uptown Records issued a 1959 recording by this group at a club on DeBaliviere called the Holy Barbarian. In 2012, Uptown Records released the CD, *Holy Barbarian– St. Louis 1959* [*Discography*]. The Holy Barbarian was the first interracial club in St. Louis and was quickly shut down by police chicanery within eight weeks. Graf played around St. Louis and worked as an instrument repairman until his death.

St. Louisan Grant Green (1935–1979) was born into a musical family. His father bought him his instruments. Listen to the *Walter Dixon Interview* to hear a description of his childhood. Influenced by two Charlies—Christian

Grant Green, 1963. *Photographer, Francis Wolff. Courtesy Mosaic Records Jazz Photography of Francis Wolff.*

(guitar) and Parker (saxophone)—Green began learning recorded solos note for note. Saxophonist Chuck Tillman was a mentor. A professional by age thirteen, Green played in his sanctified church, in rhythm and blues bands and in jazz groups. Green was heard in every type of club on both sides of the river. He recorded two albums for Delmark with Jimmy Forrest and Elvin Jones in 1959 and in 1960 with Sam Lazar, all three in Chicago.[112] Lou Donaldson discovered him in an East Side club and took him to Blue Note records in New York, where he quickly became the house guitarist. His work past 1960 is beyond the scope of this work. He is the subject of a biography by Sharony Andrews Green.[113]

The bassist on the aforementioned Forrest recording at the Barrel and on the "Night Train" recording was John Mixon (1927–1996). Mixon learned to play bass in the U.S. Army. Leaving the army in 1949, he studied in Boston for two years, joining Jimmy Forrest in St. Louis in 1951. In addition, he worked with Hugh "Peanuts" Whalum, "Foots" Goodson, John Cotter, Bob Graf and Tab Smith in St. Louis in the 1950s. He joined Lionel Hampton in 1958, returning to St. Louis for good around 1961, making one European trip with Lester Bowie [*Mixon Interview*].

Oscar Oldham was the drummer on the Forrest "Night Train" recording. Mixon thought that he was just as good as Max Roach and other great modern jazz drummers [*Mixon Interview*]. The two were in a quartet with saxophonist "Peanuts" Whalum and pianist John "Albino Red" Chapman. On May 1, 1953, Mixon dropped Chapman off at his home and was T-boned at the corner of Euclid and Highland. Oldham was killed; Peanuts's hand and arm were so severely damaged that he was hospitalized for thirty-five days.[114]

John Mixon, 1987. *Photograph by Dennis Owsley, with permission from Darryl Mixon.*

From Memphis, Tennessee, pianist, vocalist and saxophonist Hugh "Peanuts" Whalum (born 1920)[115] has entertained St. Louis audiences since 1949. His first group was called the Three Nuts. Peanuts was with Lionel Hampton in the early 1950s and has spent the rest of his life in St. Louis, mainly as a pianist-vocalist with a voice that sounds like Nat "King" Cole.

A group of St. Louis musicians who felt that Dixieland was too primitive decided to get together to provide an alternative to that style, forming an octet they called Jazz Central, based on the West Coast Dave Pell Octet.[116] The band started working at comedian Davey Bold's Celebrity Club and soon came to the attention of Bob Hyland, the general manager of **KMOX**. The group played hotels, schools and outdoor venues. They made fifty broadcasts on **KMOX** for eighteen months on Saturdays. Jazz Central acquired the Celebrity Club space, in a building at Delmar and Skinker, in 1959. The club brought in name groups headed by Al Hirt, Cannonball Adderley, Dizzy Gillespie and others.[117] Jazz Central recorded a self-produced LP called *Natural Habitat* in 1959, featuring standards and original works [*Discography*]. The album cover art featured a huge arch on the riverfront with an airplane flying through it. (The Gateway Arch project dates to 1933, with construction beginning in 1963.)

From the 1920s on, St. Louis and its environs have been the birthplace of a number of nationally known musicians who left early without making a mark. We presented some of them in chapter 2. Some others who ended up with careers on the West Coast are Cal Tjader (born 1925),[118] arranger Lennie Niehaus (born 1929),[119] trumpeter Buddy Childers (born 1926)[120] and baritone saxophonist Bobby Gordon.[121] Avant-garde vocalist Leon Thomas (born 1937 in East St. Louis) went to college in Tennessee.[122] Their work is beyond the scope of this book.

In the latter part of the 1950s, there was a lot of jazz activity in clubs that have not been mentioned in this text. Many clubs presented jazz, among them the Judge's Chambers and Harlem Club on the East Side and the Hurricane Lounge, Roma Room, the Mellow Cellar, the Paris Lounge, the Blue Flame Club and Club Manhattan in St. Louis. El Patio, the Baby Grand, Gino's, the Beaumont Bar, Nips, the 20th Century Bar and the Frolic Bar all featured modern jazz by mainly black local musicians. Until Gaslight Square, the white local musicians and black local musicians mainly played on the DeBaliviere Strip, although Gino's had modern musicians from out of town. White musicians and some black players also worked in South St. Louis at the Fallen Angel, the Club Pastime and the Playgirl.

A random act of nature, a tornado, struck the Olive and Boyle neighborhood on February 10, 1959. This brought about Gaslight Square, an entertainment district that in its heyday employed more musicians than any other place in the country [*Menne Interview*]. The national civil rights struggle was in full swing, and another war loomed on the horizon, causing a split in the country that has continued to widen until today.

Chapter 6

THE BLUE NOTE CLUB AND GASLIGHT SQUARE (1960–1969)

A force in the local jazz scene, the Blue Note Club in Centreville, Illinois, was the place where most of the name modern jazz musicians working in St. Louis hung out after hours. Started in the late 1950s by Leo Gooden, the club lasted two years after his death in 1965. Leo was a very large man who sang in the style and sound of Billie Holiday. The handpicked house band at the club was well cared for and supplied with food during the evening.[123] He respected the musicians and always paid them [*Rice-Wilson Interview*].

Leo's Five had the following personnel: Larry Prothro (trumpet), Charles "Little Man" Wright (alto and tenor sax), Hamiet Bluiett (baritone sax) or Eddie Fisher (guitar), Don James (organ) and Kenny Rice (drums). They were recorded for LG Records in 1963 [*Discography*]. Others also sat in with the band. David Sanborn played there as a teenager. A CD called *Leo's Five Direct from the Blue Note Club, East St. Louis*, issued on Ace Records (England), includes much more material from the club and the blues scene in East St. Louis. Gooden went to New York in 1963 and recorded a vocal album (LG Records) with arrangements by Oliver Nelson [*both Discography*].

Born in St. Louis and raised in Kinloch, drummer Kenny Rice (born 1942) came from a musical family. One of his drum teachers was "Lyge" Shaw. Kenny played in blues bands and then toured with Albert King. He became a member of Leo's Five after Leo Gooden spotted him in a jam session. Later, he worked on the road with Grady Tate, Nat Adderley and the Kennedy brothers, pianist Tom and bassist Ray. Kennedy also worked with guitarists Richard Martin and Eddie Fisher and with blues pianist Johnny Johnson, among others. Rice remembered playing a version of "Night in Tunisia" that lasted over an hour when Yusef Lateef and Oliver Nelson got tied up in a tenor sax battle at the Blue Note [*Rice-Wilson Interview*]. Rice has received awards from the Missouri Historical Society and the North County Arts Council as well as being an inductee into the St. Louis Jazz of Fame at the Don and Heidi Wolf Jazz Institute at Harris-Stowe University.

Organist Don James was from Crystal City and had a radio show [*Rice-Wilson Interview*]. Rice claims that James played the organ like a piano player and played so hard it was like he was attacking the organ. During the height of organist Jimmy Smith's popularity, Leo's Five opened for him in a concert in Chicago. Smith was so overcome by James's playing that he put a rider into his contract to never have another organist on any of his engagements. James died in 1967.

Saxophonist Charles "Little Man" Wright (1927–2007?) was raised in East St. Louis. Jimmy Forrest lived across the street from him; having that contact made Wright want to be a saxophonist. After mustering out of the service in 1945, Wright took lessons at the Ludwig School of Music. He played with Eddie Randle. Wright also worked with "Snookum" Russell, Tab Smith, Count Basie, B.B. King and Ray Charles in the 1950s. Sonny Rollins thought very highly of Little Man.[124]

Saxophonist David Sanborn was born in Tampa in 1945 and later lived in Kirkwood, Missouri. A professional by age fourteen, he worked with Albert King. He later went to the University of Iowa and Northwestern University. Philip Wilson took him to the Blue Note Club, where he jammed with Leo's Five [*Rice-Wilson Interview*]. Charlie Menees took him to clinics, and J.D. Parran took him to places on Gaslight Square [*Menees and Parran Interviews*]. The rest of his illustrious career is beyond the scope of this book.

The corner of Olive and Boyle was known as Greenwich Corners, named after Greenwich Village in New York. There were bars like the Gaslight and the Golden Eagle, interesting shops and residents who were somewhat more liberal than people in other parts of St. Louis. When the tornado of February 10, 1959 blew through the neighborhood, it caused such damage that the area had to start over. According to Thomas Crone's book, *Gaslight Square: An Oral History*,[125] the local merchants quickly sank their insurance payouts into refurbishing and renovating the buildings into restaurants and nightclubs. The block on Olive east of Boyle became Gaslight, and the entertainment district called "Gaslight Square" began operations.

Eddie Fisher, Kenny Rice, David Sanborn, Hamiet Bluiett and Don James. Blue Note Club, Centreville, Illinois, early 1960s. *Courtesy Kenny Rice. Permissions from Kenny Rice, David Sanborn and Hamiet Bluiett.*

Developers opened theaters, restaurants, nightclubs, antiques shops and jazz clubs. Jay and Fran Landesman, who wrote the Broadway play *The Nervous Set*, opened the Crystal Palace. Barbra Streisand and the Smothers Brothers first gained national attention at the Crystal Palace. Comedian Lenny Bruce regularly worked in Gaslight Square. Pianist Jeter Thompson called Gaslight the jewel of the city because of the variety of entertainment found there. He also said that the Gaslight Square Association required coats and ties to get into the venues [*Thompson Interview*]. The clubs on Gaslight also had a dark side: clubs that African Americans were likely to frequent were on both ends of Gaslight, not in the middle.[126]

Dixieland was heard in quite a few clubs on Gaslight Square. The Opera House had Singleton Palmer and His Dixieland Six; Bustles and Bows and the Silver Dollar had Muggsy Sprecher's Gaslighters; the Tiger's Den had Sammy Gardner's Mound City Six; and the Natchez Queen and Bustles and Bows had the St. Louis Ragtimers.

During the Gaslight days, Norman Weinstrorer's Norman label documented many groups, including one led by society bandleader Russ

David called The Four of Us. Unfortunately, according to Dan Warner, head of Gaslight Records, the tapes were scattered all over St. Louis and poorly labeled, so we have only one CD documenting his recordings during that time [*Discography*].

Singleton Palmer was one of the stars of Gaslight Square, but he worked brutal hours. He played on Gaslight from 9:00 p.m. to 1:00 a.m. and then worked as a janitor for the Chromalloy Company until 9:00 a.m. He would get home by 10:00 every morning [*Palmer Interview*]. Musicians in St. Louis have always had to work two jobs to make ends meet. Palmer's group made three recordings for Norman Records in 1961 and 1964. His band also recorded two LPs for Opera House Records in 1964 and, in 1967, one recording for the Japanese Paddlewheel label [*all Discography*].

Muggsy Sprecher (1922–1999) was from Wisconsin. He played cornet from age nine and in the military during World War II. After the war, Sprecher came to St. Louis and worked with Sammy Gardner before starting his own group. Sprecher was a favorite on Gaslight Square, but his real job was as an advertising salesman for the St. Louis Suburban Journals. He played off and on for the St. Louis Jazz Club. Sprecher's group recorded four times: three for Norman Records and one for Marbro Records [*Discography*].

Sammy Gardner (1926–1995) was born in St. Louis but studied clarinet in the Kirkwood schools. He was a professional while he was still in high school. He also played all the other woodwinds, trumpet, tuba and violin. Following military service, Gardner earned a bachelor's degree in music at the St. Louis Institute of Music. Like other St. Louis musicians, Gardner had two parallel careers: teacher and performer. He recorded with his Windy City Six for Delmar in 1953. He was on Arthur Godfrey's show in 1958, and he had his own TV show, which lasted for two years. Gardner returned to St. Louis and had a long run at Charlie Wells's Tiger's Den on Gaslight. He was known for his showmanship. Gardner trained many of St. Louis's Dixieland musicians as they passed through his group. While on Gaslight Square, Gardner recorded an LP for Norman Records and one for Paddlewheel.[127] With the demise of Gaslight Square, Gardner moved to Florida. For some funny stories about Sammy Gardner, listen to the *Joe Buerger Interview.*

A band that played pre-jazz music was the St. Louis Ragtimers. Trebor Tichenor (piano), Bill Mason (cornet), Al Stricker (banjo) and Don Franz (tuba) had a long run at the Golden Eagle (before Gaslight) and then at the Natchez Queen (1961–64) and Bustles and Bows (1964).[128] The Ragtimers made two recordings in St. Louis for GHB Records in 1963 and 1964. Tichenor's piano rolls were on a Folkways LP in 1964. He was also recorded

St. Louis Ragtimers at the Nachez Queen, 1961. *From left to right*: Don Franz, Bill Mason, Trebor Tichenor and Ed Freund. *Photograph by Bob Whiteside, with permission from Don Franz.*

playing solo piano on the *Goldenrod Showboat* for Ragophile in 1966 [*all Discography*]. The Ragtimers continue to perform today, even after the death of Tichenor in 2014.

Four jazz vocalists had most of the work on Gaslight Square. They were Ceil Clayton, Jeanne Trevor, Clea Bradford and Connie Morris. The first three made recordings, but Morris was not recorded, although she may have been the most popular on Gaslight. Trevor called her the queen of Gaslight.

Massachusetts-born Ceil Clayton was mainly a solo pianist and vocalist on Gaslight at Mr. D's Steak House. She moved to St. Louis after World War II and recorded two albums in the early 1960s [*Discography*]. Clayton started playing in a trio context in the 1980s and worked in Scandinavia late in her career. She died in 1997.[129]

Clea Bradford-Silverlight[130] was born in a small town south of Cape Girardeau, Missouri, but was schooled in St. Louis. She was a neighbor of Jimmy Forrest, who inspired her to sing. She made her debut at Faust's in East St. Louis and was then on the Playboy Club circuit.[131] She worked on

Jeanne Trevor. *Courtesy Western Historical Manuscript Collection, University of Missouri–St. Louis, UMSL Black History Project (1980–1983) Photograph Collection.*

Gaslight from 1962 to 1966 until leaving to tour nationally and settled in Washington, D.C., until her death in 1997.

A St. Louis resident since the early 1960s, singer-actress Jeanne Trevor was originally from New Jersey. While she was on Gaslight, she worked at the Dark Horse, Vanity Fair and Le Jazz Hot.[132] Around 1965, Trevor recorded an album for Mainstream Records with the Quartette Trés Bien and saxophonist "Peanuts" Whalum [*Discography*]. The rest of her illustrious career will be detailed in subsequent chapters.

All during the time of Gaslight Square, some in the police force looked askance at racially mixed couples. It was set up in an interesting way. The

The Other Side and Dark Side Clubs, Gaslight Square. *Courtesy Western Historical Manuscript Collection, University of Missouri–St. Louis, UMSL Black History Project (1980–1983) Photograph Collection.*

clubs featuring Dixieland, jazz vocalists and comedy were in the middle of the block. Three clubs that featured modern jazz —the Dark Side, the Other Side and the Club Trés Bien—were on the east end of the block, and Jorgie's was in the basement of the Adams Hotel on the west end of the block. Possibly it was a coincidence, but those clubs were the ones that attracted a black clientele. Both the Other Side and Jorgie's didn't have liquor licenses.

The first group to play the Dark Side was the Don Cunningham group. Don was born in St. Louis and took saxophone lessons with Theron Slaughter. Oliver Nelson was a good friend. After army service in Korea, Johnny Mathis hired him after he subbed in the Mathis big band at the

Chase. Mathis took him all over the country and to the Far East, where he became enamored with exotic music like that of vibes player Arthur Lyman and his recording "Quiet Village" with Martin Denny. Returning to St. Louis, he founded a group consisting of four black men playing "Hawaiian" music. The group opened the Dark Side on Gaslight Square. When Don had to go back on the road with Mathis, he recommended the Quartette Trés Bien for the Dark Side gig [*Cunningham Interview*].

After leaving Mathis, Don returned to St. Louis and eventually got a job at the Playboy Club. His quartet was himself on reeds, vibes and percussion; Marion Miller on keyboards; John Mixon on bass and cello; and Manny Quintero on drums and percussion. While they were at the Playboy Club, they recorded an album in 1965 on Exclusive Records [*Discography*]. Only five hundred copies of the album were pressed. Cunningham left for Los Angeles in the early 1970s and married Alicia Cunningham there. In 2003, one of the tunes from that recording, "Tabu," became very popular with the jazz-dance club crowd. The album became a hit on CD. Both Don and Alicia performed together until her death in 2014. They had an international reputation everywhere in the world except in the United States [*Cunningham Interview*]. Don and Alicia used to do an annual show in St. Louis.

The Quartette Trés Bien of Jeter Thompson (piano), Richard Simmons (bass), Albert St. James (drums) and Percy James (hand percussion) followed the Cunningham group into the Dark Side, and there an event happened that put them in the national spotlight. The *Route 66* television show was in

Alicia and Don Cunningham. *Courtesy Don Cunningham, with permission.*

The Quartette
Trés Bien. *Courtesy
Historical Images.com.*

St. Louis and filmed a sequence in the Dark Side with the group [*Thompson Interview*]. This eventually led to two recordings by the group on Norman Records [*Discography*]. Norman Wienstroer was instrumental in the group signing with Decca Records.

The group left the Dark Side and started Club Trés Bien on the east end of Gaslight. The December 23, 1963 *Post-Dispatch* carried an ad for the club. The group accompanied Clea Bradford and, after eight months, sold the club and went on the road under the sponsorship of Dick Gregory [*Thompson Interview*]. During the 1960s, the *Post-Dispatch* had twenty mentions of the Quartette Trés Bien. They were on the road for ten years, playing all the major venues, and recorded thirteen albums for Decca and one for Atlantic in that time. The Quartette Trés Bien came off the road in 1973, because jazz clubs were closing all over the country with no supporting circuit for travel.

Born into a musical family, St. Louisan Jeter Thompson (1930–2017) started playing the piano at age five and had formal training. He went to

Sumner High School and was a professional at sixteen. He was thrown out of school several times for playing boogie-woogie in the choir room. Jeter was the class president of the 100th class at Sumner. After the army, he returned to St. Louis in 1954 and began working in the city. The Quartette Trés Bien was formed in 1959 [*Thompson Interview*]. The rest of Thompson's career will be detailed in subsequent chapters of this book.

The Other Side was behind the Dark Side and, according to its original manager, Jorge Martinez, was operated out of a garage. It was an after-hours jazz coffeehouse that did not sell liquor. According to Martinez, they brought in a jazz trio, and the place was packed every night. For reasons that are not understood, well-known jazz DJ "Spider" Burks was moved into Martinez's spot, and the Other Side eventually closed.[133]

Martinez then opened a non-alcohol club in the Adams Hotel on the west end of Gaslight. It was called Jorgie's, Jorgie's Jazz Club or Jorgie's Hip Intertainment (depending on the source). Martinez brought world-class musicians into the club, which lasted only from May to the end of the summer of 1961. Ads in the *Post-Dispatch* detailed the impressive lineup: Johnny Hartman backed by the Andrew Hill Trio, the Montgomery Brothers, Nancy Wilson backed by the Three Sounds, the Donald Byrd–Pepper Adams Quintet and the Shirley Horn Trio with John Mixon and Gene Gammage. The club had recording equipment tied into the public address system.[134] Somehow, these private bootleg tapes, for which the musicians were not paid, made their way to VGM Records, which issued them on LPs in the 1980s [*Discography*].

Almost from its beginning, there were doubts about Gaslight Square. The *Post-Dispatch* of August 8, 1961, expressed misgivings about its possible expansion and parking. For a district that was supposed to be the crown jewel of the city, press coverage was surprisingly light, often focusing on negatives. The February 23, 1965 edition cited mounting crime concerns, a time-honored tactic to boost circulation. These concerns were addressed in an article in the November 1, 1965 edition of the paper citing a study showing that the crime ascribed to Gaslight actually occurred in the surrounding neighborhoods. Others put the decline of Gaslight Square as beginning around 1964 or 1965, when some fast-buck operators decided to bring in go-go dancers [*Thompson Interview*]. Thomas Crone noted that local hotel owners put pressure on cab drivers to not take customers to the Square because it was competition for their own entertainment rooms.[135]

The heyday of Gaslight Square lasted from about 1961 to 1964. Other events were bringing tension to the country, including the November 1963 assassination of President John Kennedy, civil rights violence, increasing involvement in the Vietnam War and the passage of the Civil Rights Act. Leo Gooden died in 1965, and the Blue Note Club began a decline that lasted until it closed in 1967. The white players moved to South St. Louis and to riverfront venues such as the *Goldenrod Showboat*. As in all such cultural upheavals, the black players had few places to practice their craft.

In 1964, Frank Pearson bought the *Goldenrod Showboat*. He also owned the Old Levee House [*Kittrell Interview*]. The St. Louis Ragtimers was the "house band" on the boat for twenty years. In 1965, Pearson and Trebor Tichenor started the National Ragtime and Traditional Jazz Festival on the *Goldenrod* over the Labor Day weekend. The festival continued in St. Charles and in 2000 at the Missouri History Museum in Forest Park until at least 2006.[136]

Pianist-vocalist Jean Kittrell (1927–2018) started working solo in St. Louis at the Old Levee House on the riverfront in 1967. At the time, she was in Carbondale, working on her PhD in English literature. She then became a professor of English literature at Southern Illinois University–Edwardsville and chaired the department for many years. She was a favorite in St. Louis Dixieland circles since 1967 and performed all over the world [*Kittrell Interview*]. Her subsequent long career will be detailed in succeeding chapters.

The *Post-Dispatch* documented many nationally known jazz musicians visiting the city at the Jazz Central Club and at Kiel Auditorium and Opera House in the 1960s. For instance, the Jazz Central Club had Cannonball Adderley, Nancy Wilson and Dizzy Gillespie with the Herb Drury Trio playing at other times in 1960 and 1961. Kiel had the Modern Jazz Quartet, Horace Silver, several Norman Granz package shows, a bicentennial jazz festival in 1966 and two George Wein package shows, one of which featured the Miles Davis "Lost Quintet" on August 16, 1969. The Mississippi River Festival on the campus of Southern Illinois University started in 1969. The Modern Jazz Quartet was heard in one of the concerts.

Miles Davis opened at the Jazz Villa on Washington Avenue downtown on May 29, 1963. A bootleg recording of that engagement also appeared on VGM Records in the 1980s [*Discography*]. Gloria Lynne, Ramsey Lewis and Lambert, Hendricks & Ross were also heard at that club. According to Austin Bealmear,[137] Jazz Villa was a fairly large venue, possibly a converted warehouse.

Gino's, on Delmar across from the Barrel, stated bringing in nationally known musicians. Starting in 1963, the club brought in Stan Getz, Herbie Mann, a tenor sax battle between Sonny Stitt and Jimmy Forrest, the Quartette Trés Bien in 1963 and 1964, Louis Jordan and the Three

Sounds in 1965. The John Coltrane Quartet engagement of January 25 to February 2, 1963, is notable in that the drummer, Elvin Jones, was late due to a delayed flight for opening night. Drummers Chauncey Williams and Phillip Wilson played two short sets. Austin Bealmear described what happened after Jones arrived:

> *You know how hard it is to describe music in words, but it was as if the history of jazz had just gone from the past to the future. You could feel the emotional change in the audience as everyone realized this was a different concept of swing and group interaction. Chorus after chorus the intensity kept building, way beyond anything I'd ever heard before.*
>
> *The only PA was one mic for Trane, and yet they were playing louder than I'd ever heard anyone. They were filling the entire room with this massive wall of sound. I could not imagine how they could get that much sound out of acoustic instruments.*
>
> *Phillip was so moved, he could not contain himself....He was kneeling at the stage in front of Elvin and beating on the stage....Just when you thought it couldn't possibly get more intense, they would turn it up another notch. Phillip (and I am not exaggerating) was running down the aisle between the bar and the tables, wailing and throwing himself up against the wall by the front door, over and over again. It was an experience I will never forget.*[138]

The Upstream Lounge opened at Seventh and Pine in 1964. Pianist Gayle Bell worked there initially and was succeeded by the Eddie Fritz Quartet, which played there for seven years [*Fritz Interview*]. Over the years, including a move to 903 West Pine, the Upstream hosted the Gordon Lawrence Latin Jazz group, the Bernard Hutcherson Quartet, the Kennedy Brothers and Stablemates with organist Benny Wilson and saxophonist Bob Gibson. Stablemates were documented in the *Post-Dispatch*. By 1978, the Upstream was out of the jazz business.

Trumpeter Webster Young was in St. Louis at Nero's on the DeBaliviere Strip in the summer of 1965. VGM Records released three LPs under his name [*Discography*]. A number of local musicians, including pianists John Hicks and John "Albino Red" Chapman and saxophonist Freddie Washington, took part in what appear to be jam sessions. The personnel on each tune is unknown. The *Lord Discography* gives personnel, but to the author, it is suspect, because the date is listed as 1961.

Born in St. Louis, Freddie Washington (born 1937) heard music around his house—his mother played piano by ear. Taken with the sound of the alto sax, he started taking lessons from Theron Slaughter, a musician who played with Eddie Randle. By the time he was sixteen, Washington was playing with Jimmy Houston's band and later with George Hudson's orchestra. He graduated from Sumner High School and joined the navy in 1956 as a musician, stationed in Washington, D.C., with the navy band. He returned to St. Louis in 1959 and began working in a quintet with Bobby Danzig, John Chapman, John Mixon and the legendary drummer Joe Charles. Freddie was also invited to audition for John Coltrane's place in the Miles Davis Quintet but turned the invitation down because he felt he wasn't ready [*Washington Interview*]. The author remembers Freddie with Mongo Santamaria in Los Angeles around 1965. Washington's influences as a saxophone player are Sonny Stitt, Stan Getz, Sonny Rollins and John Coltrane. Freddie's first recordings were for the VGM label in 1965, with Webster Young (see above). The rest of his long St. Louis career will be detailed in subsequent chapters.

Another of St. Louis's great musicians, pianist John Hicks, was born in Atlanta and moved to St. Louis in 1955 when his father became the pastor of Union Memorial Methodist Church. Hicks attended Sumner High and went to Lincoln University in 1958 for one year. He then went to New York, working with many well-known players. He attended Berklee College of Music at this time. In 1964, he joined Art Blakey. Hicks was in and out of St. Louis in the mid-1960s and eventually joined Woody Herman in 1968 [*Hicks Interview*]. One of the most in-demand pianists in jazz, Hicks's career away from St. Louis is beyond the scope of this book.

Piano legend John "Albino Red" Chapman went to Sumner High School and was in demand when he was very young. Hicks met Chapman when he tuned the Hicks family piano. The two pianists hung out a lot in the late 1950s. Hicks found him very inspiring, as did many others. Chapman, a drug user, froze to death in the winter of 1978 [*Washington Interview*].

Pianist Herb Drury was working all over St. Louis in the 1960s, and his trio with Jerry Cherry (bass) and Phil Hulsey (drums) recorded an LP for Exclusive Records in 1965 [*Discography*]. "Peanuts" Whalum also worked a lot in the '60s but did not record. The subsequent careers of these two musicians will be recounted in the following chapters.

Mr. C's La Cachette opened in Overland, a suburb of St. Louis, in 1966. Ads show that the club played host to pianist Dave Venn and saxophonist Bernard Hutcherson in the late 1960s. Graham Chapel, on the campus of Washington University, hosted a number of jazz events. The *Post-Dispatch* shows a liturgical jazz show with the St. Louis Ragtimers and the St. Louis Jazz Quartet (1962), Zoot Sims with the Herb Drury and

Left: Dave Venn, 2014. *Photograph by Dennis Owsley, with permission from Dave Venn.*

Right: John Hicks. *Courtesy of Elise Wood (widow).*

Dave Venn Trios (1963) and Roscoe Mitchell (1967). In 1966, Thelonious Monk played Graham Chapel and went to a student after-concert party (December 2, 1966).

In the 1960s, the *Post-Dispatch* printed a number of articles on jazz. Charlie Menees and Harper Barnes did record reviews and concert previews. There were the usual arguments about jazz in church, an article on Jonah Jones at the Chase Club (1962), a clinic by the North Texas State band at University City High School (1962), a profile of Lurlean Hunter (1963) and an article on the day jobs of St. Louis jazz musicians (1963). The paper also profiled Fontella Bass and her then-husband, Lester Bowie (1967), and had an opinion piece about jazz returning to its innocence. Jazz was big enough in St. Louis that a "Jazz Day" took place on the riverfront in June 1969. The event featured the Oliver Lake group, Odell Brown and the Organizers, Tom Scott and Oliver Nelson with Duke Pearson, Mickey Roker, Bob Cranshaw, Stanley Turrentine, Clea Bradford, Big John Patton and Clark Terry.

A major jazz event in St. Louis was the return of Oliver Nelson in the summers to teach and run a jazz clinic at Washington University. The *Post-Dispatch* did not list any details about the 1967 or 1968 clinics, but the 1969 one was covered extensively. There was a four-page photo spread and

Oliver Nelson at the 1969 Oliver Nelson Clinic. *Courtesy Washington University Libraries, Department of Special Collections.*

discussions of Nelson's music. There were four concerts in the Washington University quadrangle by Nelson, Phil Woods, Sir Roland Hanna, Ron Carter and Mel Lewis, who also taught in the clinics. In addition, there were concerts and clinics in communities on both sides of the river. Bob Bearman had a student big band (founded the year before) that served as the focus for the 1966 clinic; Austin Bealmear, an architecture student, was the drummer. Bealmer also played with Bernard Hutcherson at Mr. C's in 1969.

Other events that occurred in St. Louis from 1967 to 1979 will be detailed in chapter 7.

Chapter 7

THE BLACK ARTISTS GROUP (BAG), THE HUMAN ARTS ENSEMBLE AND THE COLLAPSE OF THE SCENE (1967–1979)

The years 1968–1973 were a time of protest over the war in Vietnam, over lifestyles that were very nontraditional and over other issues. The nation was split between forward-looking individuals and those trying to maintain traditional values. By 1972, the nation was gripped by a recession. The arts community was no different. In jazz, one group tried to hold on to what they perceived as the jazz tradition (i.e., Dixieland), and a second group tried to change the way music was considered. A third group, neither Dixieland nor avant-garde, was quietly doing its own thing. Recordings made in St. Louis at this time break down this way: eighteen Dixieland, five mainstream and twelve avant-garde. This reflected the split in the country, a split that continues and is magnified today [*Discography*].

With music scenes beginning to collapse by 1967, jazz musicians faced a future with few places to play. The riverfront provided a haven for the Dixieland players, with the *Goldenrod Showboat* as its focus. The Old Levee House and other entertainment venues featured jazz as a way to connect nostalgically to romantic notions about the riverboat era in St. Louis's history. The St. Louis Ragtimers played as the house band on the *Goldenrod Showboat* for twenty years. The National Ragtime and Traditional Jazz Festival was held on the *Goldenrod* every Labor Day weekend from 1965 to 1990, when it moved to St. Charles. Nearly all of the Dixieland recordings made in this period (1967–73) are out of print and unavailable [*Discography*]. See also chapter 6.

Ads in the *Post-Dispatch* detail nationally known musicians appearing at Kiel at this time, but such acts also played at the Ambassador Hotel, at Graham Chapel (New York Jazz Quartet, Roscoe Mitchell, Charles Mingus, Dexter Gordon and Johnny Griffin) and at several other colleges around St. Louis. Clubs with visiting national jazz musicians were the Gourmet Rendezvous on North Grand (Groove Holmes, Art Blakey), Helen's Black Eagle in Florissant (Sonny Stitt, Jack McDuff, Les McCann and Arthur Prysock) and La Casa on Jefferson (Sonny Stitt, Joe Williams, Horace Silver and others). The Mississippi River Festival on the campus of Southern Illinois University–Edwardsville had the Modern Jazz Quartet; a concert with McCoy Tyner, Freddie Hubbard and the group Return to Forever; and a show with Cannonball Adderley. But by 1974, visits by nationally known jazz musicians were beginning to dry up.

The mainstream jazz scene included guitarist Eddie Fisher, who was born in Arkansas. Fisher came to St. Louis with Albert King and began working at the Blue Note Club in its last years. He recorded a 45-rpm single called "Wantu Wazuri, Parts I and II" in 1968 that brought him to the attention of Cadet Records. His two Cadet albums, recorded in 1969 and 1970, were well received [*Discography*]. Fisher toured internationally but had virtually no attention in St. Louis.[139] Eddie Fisher died in 2007.

Mississippi native James "Ironhead" Matthews (born 1943)[140] began performing early in East St. Louis. Initially a drummer, he switched to piano at age seven. He was recorded with Eddie Fisher on *The Next Hundred Years* [*Discography*]. Matthews continues to work today and has toured the Middle East several times. He was an elementary school teacher.

Saxophonist Willie Akins (1939–2015) was born in Webster Groves and worked professionally in St. Louis since he was sixteen with Eddie Randle and others. As soon as Willie finished his studies at Webster Groves High School in 1957, his father drove him to New York. While there, he worked with anybody who would hire him, including a lot of organists. His father got sick in 1968, and Willie returned to St. Louis [*Akins Interview*]. Willie's St. Louis career will be explored in subsequent chapters.

A lot of St. Louis piano players, including Eddie Fritz, "Peanuts" Whalum, Herb Drury and Dave Venn, found work in restaurants, motel lounges and hotel lounges. Pianist Carolbeth True started her long St. Louis career as a solo pianist at Schneithorst's Restaurant in 1972. In 1973, her own trio was founded with bassist Eddie Randle Jr. and drummer Gary Dinkelkamp (aka Gary Dink). She is one of the most in-demand classical and jazz piano teachers in St. Louis and is a longtime member of the Webster University

Fred Tompkins. *Courtesy of Fred
Tompkins.*

music faculty. True was the rehearsal pianist–assistant music director with
the St. Louis Muny Opera for twenty years.[141]

Jeanne Trevor, one of Gaslight's favorites, helped found the St. Louis Jazz
Quartet and recorded an album, *St. Louis Jazz Quartet*, for ei Productions in
1972 [*Discography*]. According to the *Post-Dispatch*, the group made an Alaska
trip in 1973.

Another St. Louis musician who became active at this time was Fred
Tompkins. Fred is a flautist and composer who writes jazz pieces that are
mainly through-composed but interpreted with jazz phrasing. He was in
New York during this time and recorded with Elvin Jones. Fred has lived in
St. Louis since the late 1970s. His work with various groups will be detailed
in subsequent chapters.

St. Louis African American high schools in the late 1950s and early 1960s
sent many talented, forward-looking artists out into the world. These artists
included trumpeter Lester Bowie; pianist-trumpeter David Hines; trumpeter
Floyd LeFlore; woodwind player J.D. Parran; drummers Chuck Carter,
Phillip Wilson, Jerome "Scrooge" Harris and Kenny Rice; and future opera
star Grace Bumbry. Oliver Lake started playing saxophone at seventeen to
be in the school band. Julius Hemphill's wife brought him to St. Louis.

Most of these musicians made their living in rhythm and blues bands, but
such gigs do not provide a basis for stretching as an artist. With the collapse
of Gaslight Square, they had no place to go, so they started playing and
jamming anywhere they could, including Art Hill in Forest Park during the
summer. The rules apparently were that anybody who showed up got to play;
they didn't worry about whether or not they had a rhythm section. Hamiet
Bluiett stressed the importance of playing every day [*Bluiett Interview*].

Lester Bowie, 1987. *Photograph by Dennis Owsley, with permission from Deborah Bowie.*

Lester Bowie[142] (1941–1999) has been described as one of the most inventive trumpeters in jazz. His father was a well-known brass teacher who brought his family from Maryland to teach music and English. Lester got interested in trumpet at age five and made his first recording at age fifteen. He married vocalist Fontella Bass, who had a hit single, "Rescue Me." The two of them moved to Chicago.

In Chicago, Bowie was becoming increasingly involved with the forward-thinking Association for the Advancement of Creative Musicians (AACM). The St. Louis musicians visited Bowie, and on one occasion, Floyd LeFlore got a pie in the face from Lester as he came through the door [*LeFlore Interview*]. Bowie became a member of the Art Ensemble of Chicago and has since led many groups, the Brass Fantasy being the most prominent. The remainder of his career is beyond the scope of this book.

Saxophonist Oliver Lake (born 1942) was born in Arkansas but grew up in St. Louis. He graduated from Sumner High School and began his music studies late, at age nineteen. He went to Lincoln University and graduated in 1968 with a BA in music education. An award-winning experimental film, *Jazoo*, was one of his first projects after college. This unique film had music composed and performed by the Oliver Lake Art Quartet. Lake was one of the founding members of the Black Artists Group (BAG) and a founding member of the World Saxophone Quartet. His career in New York is beyond the scope of this book. He is a Guggenheim Fellow.[143]

J.D. Parran also came from Sumner High School. He became a professional musician at age fifteen. As a BAG member, he performed on several of the BAG–Human Arts Ensemble recordings. He left for New

Oliver Lake, 2006. *Photograph by Dennis Owsley, with permission from Oliver Lake.*

York in 1971, returning to St. Louis in 1973. Parran and LeFlore formed 3rd Circuit and Spirit, which had guitarist Marvin Horn among its members. He left St. Louis again in 1977 and never returned. He, too, has had a long and productive career as a saxophonist-composer.[144]

Visits by the AACM gave St. Louis musicians the idea to organize. An area called Laclede Town was beginning to be populated by leftist political activists. In that area was the Berea Presbyterian Church, which had a racially mixed congregation and theater group. Civil rights were the focal point of much of the work.

The *Post-Dispatch* lists a concert by the Oliver Lake ensemble in honor of Dr. Martin Luther King Jr. at the Sheldon Memorial on April 14, 1968. Poet, actor and stage director Malinké Elliott decided to stage Jean Genet's play *The Blacks* with music and dance integrated into the production. This was presented on August 1 and 2 at Webster College's Loretto-Hilton Theater.

Trumpeter Baikida E.J. Carroll was also involved in BAG. He went to Soldan High School and played with Lester Bowie and J.D. Parran. After military service, Carroll was working in rhythm and blues and jamming on Art Hill. He performed as an actor in *The Blacks* and became a BAG member. Carroll went to Paris in 1972 with the BAG ensemble and stayed until 1975. He has been a major musician since that time as a theater and jazz composer. That part of his career is beyond the scope of this book.[145]

In the same time period, these musicians incorporated as the Black Artists Group, Incorporated, with Julius Hemphill as chair, Malinké Elliot as artistic and executive director and Oliver Lake as treasurer. Once the group was incorporated, it obtained Rockefeller and Missouri Arts Council grants and bought a building on Washington Avenue known as "the BAG House." BAG was part of the "Black Arts" movement in the country at that time.[146]

Julius Hemphill (1938–1995) was born in Fort Worth and played with local blues and jazz bands. After college and the army, he moved to St. Louis with his wife in 1966. He was the BAG president and collaborated with other composers during this time. Julius moved to New York in 1973 (*St. Louis Post-Dispatch*, December 9, 1973) and became one of the founding members of the World Saxophone Quartet, along with Bluiett and Lake. In New York, Hemphill was involved in many multimedia endeavors beyond the scope of this book.[147]

The first BAG event that presented a large ensemble was a concert called "The Third World" at the St. Louis Art Museum on August 25, 1968. Trumpeter Floyd LeFlore described the presentation as "a multi-media type thing" [*LeFlore Interview*]. The participants included Hamiet Bluiett,

Oliver Lake and J.D. Parran (reeds); Jerome "Scrooge" Harris and Charles "Bobo" Shaw (drums); a dance troupe; and poet Ajulé (Bruce) Rutlin. The Art Museum Theater is small, and it filled quickly. The presentation was long; as people left, others claimed their seats. The concert ended with a standing ovation.

By early 1970, saxophonists Hamiet Bluiett and James "Jabbo" Ware had moved to New York and began to affect the scene there. Bluiett (1940–2018) was one of the greatest baritone sax players in jazz. He was born in St. Louis and raised in Brooklyn, Illinois. He studied under the bandleader George Hudson. He began on clarinet

Hamiet Bluiett, 2006. *Photograph by Dennis Owsley, with permission from Hamiet Bluiett.*

at age nine and took up baritone and flute while he was at Southern Illinois University. Bluiett recorded with Leo's Five at the Blue Note Club in 1963 while he was in the navy. By the late 1960s, Bluiett was playing with the musicians playing on Art Hill [*Bluiett Interview*]. He left for New York in 1969. His work away from St. Louis is beyond the scope of this book. He is best known for his work with the World Saxophone Quartet and his groups the Clarinet Family and Four Baritone Band.[148]

The musician's collectives of BAG, the AACM and Detroit often exchanged groups. BAG was different than these other groups, because it often incorporated dance, poetry and painting into its presentations. It also was teaching the arts in a community school at the BAG House. BAG had at least ten groups allied with it: the Children of the Sun, the BAG Big Band, Red Black & Green Solidarity Unit, Fire-Earth-Air-Water, Omawali Dancers, Malinque Rhythm Tribe, the BAG Drama Department, the Great Black Music Orchestra of St. Louis, the Julius Hemphill Quartet and Oliver Lake's groups. These groups presented concerts at universities, the BAG House and the Gateway Theater. BAG presented thirty consecutive weeks of concerts in 1969.[149]

According to Benjamin Looker, at its height, the BAG community school had more than two hundred students studying music, theater, poetry, dance and visual arts. Among the students were Bruce Purse, George Sams and

Ronnie Burrage. *Courtesy Ronnie Burrage, with permission.*

Ronnie Burrage, who went to New York in 1976 and has played with just about everybody. He has his own studio and teaches at Pennsylvania State University.[150]

Another was reed player Marty Ehrlich (born 1955), born in St. Paul, Minnesota, and raised in University City. He heard recordings of people like Ornette Coleman, John Coltrane and Albert Ayler in a ninth-grade theater class taught by Malinké Elliott. Ehrlich made his first recordings with the Human Arts Ensemble. He went to the New England Conservatory and moved to New York in 1978 and has forged a long progressive career that is still going today.[151]

The *Post-Dispatch* mentioned Oliver Lake's activities several times in 1970–73. BAG had a month of concerts at the Sheldon Memorial in February 1970. Julius Hemphill presented a concert at Forest Park Community College on July 19, 1970. There was also an article on Hemphill the day before. The paper also reported on BAG giving free concerts for kids in the neighborhoods sponsored by the Mayor's Council on Youth. Most of the musicians in BAG were not concerned with political activism; the music always came first.

BAG had no problems working with like-minded white or integrated arts groups.[152] The Human Arts Association was formed in 1970. Ajulé Rutlin and the white saxophonist James Marshall, among others, founded

Marty Ehrlich. *Photographer unknown. Courtesy Marty Ehrlich.*

the group. Marshall's wife, Carol, and drummer Charles "Bobo" Shaw also joined the group, which performed under the name Human Arts Ensemble. Carol had some money from a trust fund and insurance and used it to pay for the Human Arts Ensemble recordings. After their sojourn in Oregon (see below), Marshall and Carol returned to St. Louis and had two children; they divorced in 1979.[153]

Also in 1971, a contingent of several members of the Human Arts Association, the Marshalls, saxophonist Luther Thomas, bassist Arzina Richardson and Ajulé Rutlin found a place to set up an artist colony in Creswell, Oregon. According to Thomas, they were able to intersect with advanced musicians on the West Coast, inspiring them to continue their work.

Community radio station KDNA became an outlet for the BAG–Human Arts Ensemble music. It certainly was something most of the Greater St. Louis populace had not heard before. BAG poet Michael Castro started a monthly poetry and music show that ran for three years.[154]

Although BAG members appeared sporadically on a KMOX-TV show called *Heads Up*, which started in 1969, print media and the other TV outlets were either indifferent or hostile toward the music. Like all advanced musicians, there were accusations that none of the BAG people could play [*LeFlore Interview*].

The African Continuum presented a 1971 concert called "Images: Sons/Ancestors" at Powell Symphony Hall. This was a collaboration among Julius Hemphill, poet Michael Harper and visual artist Oliver Jackson. The concert was advertised in the *Globe-Democrat* and the *Argus*. The concert was also previewed. St. Louis has always neglected its local artists, and the preview was no exception. Harper was from outside St. Louis and had published a critically acclaimed book of poetry. The St. Louis artists had only a few sentences out of a large half-page article on Harper. Despite being interrupted by a bomb threat, the concert went on. Hemphill led a ten-piece orchestra through various jazz styles. The group included Hemphill, Willie Akins and J.D. Parran (reeds), Zak Diouf and Ishaq Rajab (trumpet), Victor Reef (trombone), John Hicks (keyboards), Abdul Wadud (cello), Mor Thiam (percussion) and Phillip Wilson (drums).

The twelve recordings of BAG and the Human Arts Ensemble are very hard to find. Most of these recordings feature small percussion instruments and unusual ensembles [*Discography*]. These recordings reflect the times, with a number of styles in use at the time; jazz-rock, free jazz, free-bop, trance music, "world music," rhythm and blues and the "energy music" of

Albert Ayler. After the breakup of BAG in 1973, the BAG–Human Arts Ensemble musicians made several more recordings until around 1980. The later recordings have been reissued on Freedonia Music.

Of special mention is the 1972 recording "Dogon A.D." by the Julius Hemphill Quartet of Baikida Carroll (trumpet), Hemphill (alto sax), Abdul Wadud (cello) and Phillip Wilson (drums). This recording has been lauded as a "classic" free jazz recording. The title has to do with the Dogon people of Africa, who started performing some of their dances for the tourist trade. The A.D. stands for "Alternative Dance" [*Hemphill Interview*]. The recording was on Hemphill's Mbari label and later was released by Arista. Malinké Elliot told the author that the rhythm of "Dogon" came from an Appalachian fiddler.[155] Rhythm and blues saxophonist Oliver Sain engineered and produced the recording.

By late 1972, there were signs that a recession was coming. For BAG, funding sources were drying up. These stresses caused BAG to come apart due to the disappearing finances and philosophical/political differences that caused various parts of the organization and individuals to go their separate ways. Oliver Lake; Lester Bowie's brother, trombonist Joseph Bowie; Baikida Carroll; Floyd LeFlore; and Bobo Shaw formed an ensemble that eventually obtained enough money to get to Paris, along with two vans for traveling around France. They left in late October and got a surprise when they arrived in Paris. They were asked to appear on French television and played in many concerts [*LeFlore Interview*]. The BAG ensemble recorded in 1973 [*Discography*]. Only about one hundred LPs were pressed, so this one is the rarest of the rare. LeFlore, Bowie and Shaw returned to St. Louis, but Lake and Carroll remained for two more years, teaching and recording. When they returned to the United States, they went to New York.

People from the BAG theater organization—Malinké Elliot and his wife, actress Portia Hunt, and costume designer Darryl Harris—moved to Sweden and formed a theater company. Julius Hemphill followed that same year. Hemphill visited the BAG ensemble musicians in Paris in 1973, returned to St. Louis for a short time and then moved to New York.[156] The *Post-Dispatch* had a story on Hemphill moving to New York in its December 9, 1973 edition.

What did BAG and the Human Arts Association accomplish for St. Louis and the outside world? Without these organizations, the work of Lester Bowie, Julius Hemphill, Oliver Lake, Hamiet Bluiett, J.D. Parran and Baikida E.J. Carroll would be just that of local musicians scuffling to get gigs and playing music they had to play and not music they wanted to play.

Without the influx of these and many other musicians from the Midwest into New York, the music might not have changed and evolved. According to the composer Anthony Davis, the influx of musicians from St. Louis and Chicago to New York changed the music practices of the more forward-looking musicians in New York for at least twenty years [*Davis Interview*]. In St. Louis, after BAG dissolved, two-thirds of the jazz recordings were Dixieland or ragtime [*Discography*].

The black and white unions in St. Louis remained segregated, even though the American Federation of Labor ordered the merger of all segregated unions. In St. Louis, both musicians' unions voted against a merger. The American Federation of Musicians re-ordered a merger in 1971.[157] However, the new union would not order its members to stop discriminatory hiring practices [*Hines Interview*]. Picketing by black union members led to auditions for theater orchestras held with musicians playing behind curtains. In the merger, the black musicians' union hall was sold. The money from the sale and the treasury of the black union disappeared [*Randle Interview*].

In the *Post-Dispatch*, there was the yearly story on the National Ragtime and Traditional Jazz Festival. If mentions in the paper are an indication of the popularity of an individual or an institution, it is clear where the majority of St. Louis jazz was heading. Jeanne Kittrell had 51 mentions and the *Goldenrod Showboat* 917 mentions in the years 1974–79. Of special note is Greg Franzwa's Tiger Rag Forever Jazz Band, which had a mixture of professionals and amateurs, including the cornet player, William A. Wilkinson, the head librarian at Monsanto Corporation.

The minority of jazz recordings made in the period fit the "mainstream" category [*Discography*]. Trombonist Jimmy Haislip and guitarist Bobby Caldwell (a country and western player) recorded with Herb Drury, Jerry Cherry and drummer John Brophy. The Kenny Rice–Richard Martin Quartet with Ray and Tom Kennedy and Freddie Washington backed Nat Adderley on a recording made on the campus of Southern Illinois University–Edwardsville. Buddy Emmons, a pedal steel guitar wizard, recorded a jazz album at the Chase Park Plaza Hotel; the Gateway City Big Band recorded LPs in 1977 and 1979; and Eddie Fisher was recorded in East St. Louis. Longtime vocalist and club owner Gene Lynn was recorded as well. None of these ephemera is available except *The Kenny Rice Quartet with Special Guest Nat Adderley* (Autumn Hill Records).

The Kennedy brothers, pianist Ray (1957–2015) and bassist Tom (born 1960), graduated from Maplewood High School and had strong careers both inside and outside of St. Louis. Ray was John Pizzarelli's pianist for many years until 2006, when he fell ill.[158] Tom also moved to New York and played with many bands through his long career. Tom is still working and teaching in New York. They have made several recordings together [*Discography*].

Ray and Tom Kennedy. *Courtesy Tom Kennedy.*

Asa Harris, an extraordinary vocalist, moved to St. Louis in 1973. Her father was the pianist-vocalist Ace Harris, and her uncle was trumpeter and bandleader Erskine Hawkins, who was known in the swing era as the "Twentieth-Century Gabriel." She worked with trumpeter Joe Bozzi and then with Eddie Fritz at the Breckenridge and then the Upstream until it closed (*Post-Dispatch*, December 1978, February 1978 and March 1978). Her further St. Louis career will be detailed in chapter 8.

Alto saxophonist Greg Osby was born in St. Louis in 1960. He started playing saxophone in 1974. Soon, he was playing in blues and rhythm and blues bands. He was exposed to Charlie Parker at sixteen and, in 1978, went to Howard University to study jazz. He attended the Berklee College of Music (1980–83) and moved to New York, starting the M-Base collective in 1985. His further career is beyond the scope of this book.[159]

Asa Harris Finley, 1999. *Photograph by Martin Schweig Studio, with permission from Asa Harris Finley.*

Toward the end of the 1970s, the idea of jazz education, long talked about by Charlie Menees and others, was coming to the forefront. The Stan Kenton band visited and ran clinics at Parkway and University City High Schools (1972). University City High School also hosted the Don Ellis (1971) and Count Basie bands (1974?). Guitarist-composer Steve Schenkel started the Webster College (now university) jazz department in 1979. It started a concert series featuring local and, occasionally, national musicians that

Left: Greg Osby. *Photographer unknown. Courtesy Greg Osby, with permission.*

Right: Steve Schenkel (*left*) and Willem von Hombracht, 2011. *Photograph by Dennis Owsley, with permissions from Steve Schenkel and Willem von Holmbracht.*

continues to the present day [*Post-Dispatch*]. That same year, trombonist Brett Stamps stared the jazz department at Southern Illinois University–Edwardsville.

The 1970s was a "golden age" of jazz radio in St. Louis. This is how things came to be. The first all-jazz show goes back to 1945, when writer and jazz fan Charlie Menees started his first show on WTMV in East St. Louis. Charlie was a beloved, very sentimental man who was on WIL (1949), KWMU (1971–78) and KMOX (1978–93). He played mostly swing, traditional and Dixieland jazz but was excoriated by his audience for playing the first bebop recordings in St. Louis [*Menees Interview*].

Wiley Price was the first black disc jockey in St. Louis. He started at WTMV in 1944 and played rhythm and blues mixed with a little jazz. Jesse "Spider" Burks came to KXLW in 1946. He was then on KSTL until 1961. After a stint at KATZ, Burks went to KXLW/KADI-FM (1964–69). Harry Frost had a program called *Fresh Air* on KXLW in 1953. George Logan was heard on KXLW (1952–56, 1961–64) and KATZ (1958).[160]

In 1962, Leo Chears, known as "The Man in the Red Vest," started on WBBR in 1962, then WAMV in 1964. He was on KADI-FM (1964–68), KSD (1968–72), WMRY (1974–86), WRTH (1986), KATZ-AM and FM

(1987) and WSIE (1994–2005). In addition to bringing jazz, Chears was a poet, broadcasting some of that work. Bandleader Buddy Moreno was on KWK (1961–68), WEW (1981–90) and WSIE (1994–?). Moreno died at age 103 in 2015.

Had it not been for Menees, jazz would not have been on KWMU (now St. Louis Public Radio) since 1971. When Menees left for KMOX, Romondo Davis and then Jim Wallace broadcast the jazz program. The author came on the air in 1983 and is now in his thirty-sixth consecutive year broadcasting jazz. Around 1985, WSIE at Southern Illinois University–Edwardsville became the first full-time St. Louis jazz station, but it was a very loose situation with students and professionals. In addition to Leo Chears and Buddy Moreno, here are some who have come and gone: Jim Bohlen, Ross Gentille (1988–2013), Pat Graney (1987–96), Don Wolff (1990–93), Maria Keena, Bob Bennett, Edie Bee and LaVerne Holiday. Finances have always been a problem for the station. The station went off an all-jazz format around 2008 but has been coming back with general manager Greg Conroy and the new general manager, Jason Church (KCLC, 1998–2002; WSSM, 2001–05; KFTK, 2008–18). Maria Keena also started KZJZ in 2000, an AM jazz station that lost sponsorship over the next two years. Josh Weinstein started his show *All Soul, No Borders* in 2000 on KDHX. The show continues today.

Don Wolff, a well-known criminal defense attorney, was a jazz fan. He was on WSIE (1990–93) and, when Charlie Menees died, moved to KMOX-AM (1993–2008). By then, KMOX began trying to attract a younger audience, causing Wolff to move to KFUO-FM until it became a religious station in 2010. He also hosted a series of television shows called *I Love Jazz* on HECT-TV.

In the 1975–79 period, the *Post-Dispatch* had many references to Freddie Washington, David Hines and Asa Harris; fourteen references to Willie Akins; and six mentions of Mae Wheeler, all mainly in the 1978–79 period. The scene began to pick up again after 1979. One of the things we will see in succeeding chapters is the number of ads and articles on venues and musicians. An argument can be made that there is a strong correlation between the number of mentions in the media and the success of local venues and, possibly, local musicians.

Chapter 8

THE REVIVAL OF THE SCENE
(1980–1995)

The period from 1980 to 1995 was a slow rebuilding of the scene. Venues and institutions that featured jazz mainly came and went, but some remained in business for years. One example was the Moose Lounge in North St. Louis. If mentions in the newspaper or placings in the community calendars are any indication of the health and stability of a venue, the Moose Lounge was very successful, having more than 300 mentions in the *Post-Dispatch* from its opening in 1978 to its closing in 1999. The St. Louis Jazz Club and its Dixieland orientation had more than 150 mentions (1980–89) and 110 mentions (1990–99). On the other hand, Marquette's on Laclede's Landing had fewer than 5 mentions and lasted only a short time. So there is a correlation between the number of media mentions and the health and longevity of a venue. What about mentions of the local musicians? Paul DeMarinis, Freddie Washington, Asa Harris, Eddie Fritz, Herb Drury, David Hines and Jeanne Trevor, among others, had many mentions in this period. All have or have had successful careers in St. Louis.

A part of the problem of going to venues that feature jazz is the racial segregation endemic to St. Louis. Since the turn of the twentieth century and probably before, St. Louis has buried the areas where African Americans have lived in the name of civic progress (i.e., providing a place for white development). We have mentioned Chestnut Valley (under Union Station,

Kiel Auditorium and Busch Stadium) and Mill Creek Valley (north along Jefferson). Both were thriving communities with their own business- and professional people (doctors, lawyers, etc.). Today, the demographic of the city's north side is mainly African American. For years, the police, whether by fiat or by custom, have kept black St. Louisans more or less confined to their own neighborhoods.

St. Louis City separated from St. Louis County in 1877. Today, the county has seventy-one cities, eighteen villages and nineteen named, unincorporated areas that have their own governments, police forces and overlapping fire and school districts. For much of the twentieth century, these tiny areas were enclaves for black and white citizens, with police forces keeping blacks in their own communities. This came about in what may best be described as a real estate scam. Visit the websites in the Notes section for much more detail on the persecution of St. Louis County's black citizens in these small communities.[161] Since the advent of Grand Center with the Fox Theater, Powell Hall, the Sheldon Concert Hall, Jazz at the Bistro (1995–present) and the Kranzberg Arts Center (2008–present), people of all colors have a place to go for world-class music and theater.

In St. Louis, there seems to be a festival for everything during the year. Jazz festivals have not fared as well. In 1969, there was a St. Louis Jazz Day on the riverfront, but there were no jazz festivals after that other than the Ragtime Festival on the *Goldenrod Showboat* for twelve years. However, in the 1980s, a number of jazz festivals started happening. Charlie Wells, former owner of the Tiger's Den on Gaslight Square, started the Mid-America Jazz Festival in March 1981. That festival, with both Dixieland and swing styles, ran for eighteen years. Wells also started the Lake of the Ozarks Jazz Festival with Charlie Menees

Jo Ann Collins had a big hand in the Monsanto Jazz Festival on the riverfront in 1987 and the St. Louis Jazz Festival at Keiner Plaza in 1988 and at Washington University in 1989. For a while, the author was a part of her organization, the first Jazz St. Louis, bringing in such artists as David Murray, Oliver Lake and Bobby Watson. Richard Henderson and James Warfield started the Crusaders for Jazz organization around 1989. This group sporadically produced several concerts featuring national musicians into the mid-2000s. The organization had a mentoring and scholarship program as well.

The *Post-Dispatch* documented an astounding lineup of mainstream and avant-garde jazz musicians at the 1989 Fair St. Louis, booked by Chris Mullin and Phillip Wilson. The lineup included the Lester Bowie Brass

Freddie Washington and Sue Beshears at Monsanto Jazz Festival, 1988. *Photograph by Dennis Owsley, with permission from Freddie Washington and Sue Beshears.*

Fantasy, the Tony Williams Group, the St. Louis Jazz All-Stars, the Phillip Wilson Big Band, Emily Remler, Tania Maria and the Timeless All-Stars. Cecil Taylor was scheduled to perform but missed his airline connections and ended up at the Moose Lounge. With this one exception in 1989, jazz has been underrepresented at Fair St. Louis.

In order for a musician to be successful in St. Louis, he or she must recognize that they are independent contractors, with all of the hassles of running a small business. Showing up on time and getting a contract with the venue to protect oneself are two of the essential requirements for the operation of a small business that has the odds stacked against it—and they are stacked pretty high. Since the black and white musicians' unions were forced to combine in 1971, Local 2-197 has neglected nearly all the musicians not associated with the symphony, leading to a number of practices that have kept their pay low.[162] According to David Hines, one tactic is to allow musicians only one night per week in their venues [*Hines Interview*]. So, if you want to work five nights a week, you have to work in five different establishments. This keeps the groups from developing a following, meaning they can't ask for more money. Another tactic practiced by some of the musicians themselves is to go to a club owner and offer to play at a reduced price (in the 1920s, this was called "job knocking."). Dixieland musicians must either tour or rely on the St. Louis Jazz Club for work. A contract between the musician and club owner would help both sides. David Hines always insisted on contracts, and he worked as much as he wanted.

In order to make a decent living as a musician in St. Louis, you need a "day job." With the rise in jazz education, musicians can teach in schools, colleges and universities. The college and university jazz teachers in St. Louis are all working musicians, so they can live a somewhat comfortable, if not hectic, life.

Places to play are also important in the life of a working musician. The newspapers documented Helen's Black Eagle, the Gourmet Rendezvous and La Casa in the early 1980s. The Moose Lounge hired local and some national musicians until it closed in 1999. Mississippi Nights, Marquette's and the *Admiral* presented some local and national jazz musicians on Laclede's

Eddie Fritz. *Courtesy of Debbie Fritz (widow).*

Landing in the 1980s. Only Mississippi Nights continues to present some jazz. Other clubs that were open briefly during this period were Ice's Jazz Plus on Natural Bridge, Connors Jazz House and Major Beaux. Spruill's on Jefferson, Washington University's Holmes Lounge Jazz Series and the Webster University Jazz Series present both local and, occasionally, national jazz musicians in concert. Asa Harris and Eddie Fritz played at the Breckenridge in Frontenac for at least three years.

The press is also part of the equation for local musicians. For instance, the Webster College (now University) jazz series was started in 1980. The *Globe-Democrat* ran previews and reviews of these concerts by Tom McDermott and John McGuire until it went out of business in 1986. Some musicians religiously inform the *Riverfront Times* of their gigs. The *Post-Dispatch* ran previews of jazz events by Terry Perkins, Michael Renner and others, but no reviews have been found. With the revenue losses in print media in the digital age, these previews started drying up and seem to have disappeared after the "Great Recession" of 2008. In the 1980s, Terry Perkins profiled Dave Venn (September 17, 1985), Paul DeMarinis (November 25, 1985), David Hines (November 27, 1986), Tracer (April 23, 1987), Gene Lynn and his club (December 10, 1987), Freddie Washington (September 10, 1988), the Jimmy Williams–Henry Ettman duo (December 8, 1988), Gordon Lawrence and Con Alma (February 2, 1989) and a concert by Asa Harris at Webster University (March 30, 1989).

Increasingly, jazz education has become important in introducing the music to young people. In 1950, Charlie Menees gave a talk on jazz education in schools at a St. Louis music teachers' meeting at University City High School [*Menees Interview*]. Although "stage bands" have been in high schools since the mid-1950s, jazz education flew under the radar in St. Louis until 1972. That year, the Young Audiences program brought jazz to children all over the St. Louis area when Jeanne Trevor and the St. Louis Jazz Quartet began to do presentations for the organization. For a while in the 1970s, pianist Jimmy Williams presented jazz history programs over the public television station, KETC. Since the 1990s, "The Jazz Story" is presented to children several times a year at the Sheldon Concert Hall. Vocalists Jeanne Trevor and, more recently, Mardra Thomas and Anita Jackson along with pianist Carolbeth True and her group play to about 7,500 young people annually. Since its inception, Jazz at the Bistro (now Jazz St. Louis) has had an education wing. Its work will be detailed in chapter 10.

By the early 1980s, the idea of jazz education started to bubble up, starting at the college level and eventually working its way into high school and junior high music programs. There was also a push for jazz education among adults. Currently, Webster University and Southern Illinois University–Edwardsville have jazz studies departments. The University of Missouri–St. Louis has a jazz program led by Jim Widner, who retired in 2018. Music majors at Washington University can only minor in jazz. This has allowed our St. Louis musicians to teach young players and pass along their knowledge.

But jazz playing in public and private schools today is problematic, with funding cuts because of general disinterest in all of the arts. It is important that jazz teachers in schools have performance experience. It cannot be taught out of a textbook. Gloria Taylor's organization, Community Women

Against Hardship, was started in 1988. It now has a unique music program for fifth to twelfth graders called the Institute for the Advancement of Jazz Study and Performance. The students are taught by performing musicians.

Charlie Menees's lifelong commitment to jazz eventually gave him the idea to teach short courses to adults on jazz and big bands at a variety of venues. The 1970s and early 1980s preceded the reissue business, so he had recordings that the author had only read about. Several of his students, including the author, Don Wolff and Robert Carlock, began teaching short courses by the late 1980s.

There were a number of Dixieland and ragtime recordings made in this time. The number of these records shows the devotion to the music by both listeners and musicians. Pianist-vocalist Jean Kittrell recorded with the Old St. Louis Levee Band (1981), the Jazz Incredibles (1984) and twice with her St. Louis Rivermen (1984 and 1994). Eric Sager's Hot Jazz Band recorded in 1980. The St. Louis Ragtimers recorded three times (1981, 1988 and 1992). Ragtime pianist Trebor Tichenor recorded two CDs in 1994. Pianists Tom McDermott and John Hancock made two recordings (1981 and 1982). Hancock became a Republican politician. A reconstituted Dixie Stompers made recordings in 1993 and 1994. Trombonist Norman Menne recorded in 1985. His pianist, Pat Joyce, recorded the next year. See the *Discography* for details of each recording. In addition, there were four recordings made in St. Louis by Dixieland musicians from Chicago.

Michele Isam (reeds and vocal) and Carol Schmidt (piano and vocal) formed a very popular duo called Jasmine in late 1979. They recorded three times, in 1980, 1984 and 1986, for Sweater Records [*Discography*].

There were several "kicks" bands in St. Louis in this period. The personnel in such bands are mainly music teachers who want to keep their reading and, sometimes, their improvising skills sharp. The Gateway City Big Band was formed in 1966 and fifty-two years later is going strong. They recorded three LPs in the 1980–95 period [*Discography*]. During this period, they

Carol Schmidt, 2003. *Photograph by Dennis Owsley, with permission from Carol Schmidt.*

were mainly a swing band, but in later years they have been morphing into a jazz band. On the East Side, drummer Stan Fornaszewski led a big band that recorded two titles in 1991 and 1994. We will deal with the scope of these bands in chapter 10.

Mainstream jazz recordings were also made in St. Louis during this time. Tenor saxophonist Billy Williams and the Kennedy brothers made two recordings (1980 and 1982). Guitarist Eddie Fisher also made two recordings on the East Side. The Miller-Eaton Duo (pianist Marion Miller and vocalist Eddie Eaton) made a recording of romantic standards in 1984. Another duo, guitarist Steve Schenkel and pianist Dave Venn, recorded live at Webster University (1984). The group Left Lane with Ray Kennedy (keyboards), Peter Mayer (vocal, guitar), Jim Mayer (bass) and Roger Guth (drums) recorded in 1985. Pianist Chris Walters recorded an LP in two sessions, partly at Webster University, in 1990 and 1992. The Dan Rubright Group recorded a cassette in 1989.

Trombonist John Wolf's CD was recorded partly at the Great Grizzly Bear nightclub (1993). Pianist Herb Drury and bassist Jerry Cherry, a duo since the late 1950s, made two CDs in 1994 and 1995, while pianist Carolbeth True made her recording debut in 1994. Vocalist Michelle Shaheen made her first and only recording in 1994, while the producer of the Sheen CD, bassist Jay Hungerford, recorded a CD featuring duets with fifteen of St. Louis's finest jazz pianists [*all Discography*]. Vocalist Mae Wheeler ("Lady Jazz") was active but had no mentions in the *Post-Dispatch* and made no recordings.

University City High School had jazz bands that produced several nationally known musicians in the 1980s and early 1990s. John Brophy directed the band when it performed at the Montreux Jazz Festival in 1986. Later, David Hines directed the band. These nationally known musicians include trumpeter Jeremy Davenport, pianist Peter Martin, bassists Christopher Thomas and Neal Caine and saxophonist Todd Williams. In 1986, the

Jay Hungerford, 2010. *Photograph by Dennis Owsley, with permission.*

Above: Jeremy Davenport, 2001. *Photograph by Dennis Owsley, with permission from Jeremy Davenport.*

Left: Christopher Thomas, 2014. *Photograph by Dennis Owsley, with permission from Christopher Thomas.*

jazz band played at the Montreux Jazz Festival and was the subject of a documentary on public television station KCET called *Brophy and the Band*.

University City tenor saxophonist Todd Williams recorded an LP (1987) [*Discography*] with some other University City students, Jeremy Davenport (trumpet), Peter Martin (piano), David Berger (drums) and Mark Peterson (bass). All of these musicians, including bassist Christopher Thomas, have had long and successful careers in jazz. Williams played and recorded with Wynton Marsalis and the Lincoln Center organization. He now teaches at Indiana Wesleyan University. Jeremy Davenport worked with Harry Connick Jr. and now lives in New Orleans, where he plays and records. Davenport has a long-standing Thanksgiving gig at Jazz at the Bistro. Peterson, Berger and Thomas are part of the New York jazz scene.

Drummer Dave Weckl is from St. Charles, Missouri, and was a student of Joe Buerger, among others. After college, he became one of the top jazz-rock fusion drummers by the mid-1980s. He worked with Chick Corea for seven years and is a top studio musician, in addition to leading the Dave Weckl Band.[163] He grew up with pianist Jay Oliver, who is now a major producer in Los Angeles.[164]

Bassist Kent Miller is a graduate of Rockhurst University and also attended the University of Missouri Conservatory of Music. He returned to St. Louis and started bass studies with Warren Clauch (St. Louis Symphony) and Wendell Marshall. He played around St. Louis, including time with George Hudson. Miller went to New York in 1984 and eventually moved to Silver Springs, Maryland, where he continues to work.[165]

Peter Martin played with Joshua Redman and Betty Carter and now is the musical director and pianist for Dianne Reeves. He arranged, played music for and appeared with Reeves in the motion picture *Good Night, and Good Luck*. He now lives in University City, has a successful music series at the Sheldon and founded Peter Martin Music and the jazz teaching site Open Studio.[166]

Bassist Neal Caine is another University City High School graduate. He moved to New Orleans in 1991 to study with Ellis Marsalis. He spent five years with Elvin Jones, starting in 1994. He worked with Betty Carter and, in 2000, joined the Harry Connick Jr. Band. He is often seen on Connick's television show. He lives in New York and New Orleans.[167]

One of the most in-demand saxophonists, Chris Cheek (born 1968), was born in St. Louis, attended Webster University and then moved on to the Berklee College of Music in Boston. He moved to New York in 1992.[168]

The Bosman twins, Dwayne and Dwight, are the sons of Lloyd Smith. Born in 1953, they were going into clubs with their father by age ten and

Peter Martin. *Photograph by Dave Frenzia. Courtesy Peter Martin.*

were jamming in these clubs at fourteen. After high school, they went to Florida A&M (1971–75) and gigged around Florida for five years. They returned to St. Louis in 1980 and sewed up the job at the Moose Lounge, which they held until 1995.[169] Their long careers will be detailed in chapters 9 and 10.

Ron Carter directed East St. Louis Lincoln High School's music program, which won many regional and national honors, before moving to Northern Illinois University. This program produced musicians such as pianist Reggie Thomas, Tony Suggs, trumpeter Russell Gunn, saxophonist Andre Roberson and drummers Terreon "Tank" Gulley and Montez Coleman. Thomas is an in-demand accompanist who now heads the music department at Northern Illinois University.[170] He is the husband of vocalist Mardra Thomas. Gunn often works at the edge of jazz and hip-hop and now lives in Atlanta.[171] Both Gulley[172] and Coleman[173] work in New York, but Coleman has moved back to St. Louis. Suggs was the pianist for the Count Basie Orchestra and has produced instructional videos.[174] Roberson records in the smooth jazz genre.[175]

Quiet as it was kept, there were remnants of avant-garde music during the politically conservative 1980s. Jay Zelinka, a reed player who made his recording debut with James Marshall and the Human Arts Ensemble, formed a partnership with keyboardist Greg Mills, forming the group Exiles. Mills also recorded a solo piano album in 1984. The Exiles and Mills recordings are now available on Fredonia Music. There are eight of them from this period [*Discography*].

During the 1980s, BAG students Bruce Purse[176] (trumpet, arranger) and Kelvyn Bell (guitar) moved to New York [*Bell Interview*]. A student from Normandy High School, saxophonist Eric Person left St. Louis in 1982 and leads his groups Meta-Four and Metamorphosis.[177] Highly regarded vocalist Joan Bouise, originally from New Orleans, moved to New York in the late 1980s. She died in 1999.[178]

Pianist David Parker was experimenting with new forms during the second part of the decade.[179] He recorded three LPs in 1986, 1988 and 1989. He also recorded three albums of what he called the "November sessions" in 1988. Of these, *Stella by Flashlight* is one of only two recordings made by trumpeter David Hines. Parker's more "inside" recordings, made in 1992, are the only recordings of trumpeter Sue Beshears, the late saxophonist Jimmy Sherrod and the late, legendary drummer Joe Charles. Up-and-coming saxophonist Dave Stone also participated in these recordings. Parker also made a piano trio recording with bassist Eric Markowitz[180] and drummer Gary Sikes (1992) and another trio with Stone (1993). That one was sixty minutes of free improvisation [*all Discography*].

Dave Stone moved with his military family to St. Louis in 1989.[181] While still a student, he recorded with Parker (see above). He is one of the few free jazz saxophonists left in St. Louis. His career will be detailed in the next two chapters.

Floyd LeFlore was a trumpeter who was part of BAG in the late 1960s and early 1970s. He was part of the contingent that went to Europe. After Floyd came home, he performed sporadically. In 1993, he subbed in the Sun Ra Arkestra in a concert at the Sheldon Concert Hall. In 1994, he recorded the four-part *City Sidewalk Street Song* with tenor saxophonist John Norment [*Discography*]. LeFlore died in 2014.

In 1993, alto saxophonist Chad Evans recorded *Takin' Place* in Nashville, Tennessee, only available as a cassette [*Discography*]. Tenor saxophonist Freddie Washington made his only recording as a leader on Oliver Lake's Passin' Thru label in 1995. The CD was recorded in New York [*Discography*].

In 1988, a man from Texas, Frankie Richardson, got many black players under contract as the Lakeside All-Stars, putting on two concerts. The first concert was somewhat successful; the second was a financial disaster for both Richardson and the musicians. Richardson put ads in the media and handbills in the black community for the first concert.

The second concert received little or no publicity anywhere because Richardson could not make up his mind as to what to do, even though he had discussed his venture with professional publicists. Richardson quickly left town.

The loss of trumpeter-pianist David Hines (July 18, 1942–July 19, 1991) in a motorcycle accident near his home shocked and saddened the entire St. Louis music community. Tributes to him went on for weeks. David was originally a pianist; since his family had no piano, he practiced in the parlor of the Randle and Sons Funeral Home on Natural Bridge.[182] After he graduated from Sumner High School, Hines studied formally in several colleges and universities. David started playing trumpet in the early 1960s. By 1963, he was touring on trumpet with rhythm and blues bands in both the United States and Europe. In 1968, he was the trumpet soloist for Woody Herman and held the same position with Ray Charles in 1970. He also played in theater orchestras in St. Louis. David taught at BAG and in various school situations and led the University City High School jazz band in the late 1980s. Hines toured Europe with Lester Bowie's Brass Fantasy in the winter of 1986 and recorded with the Julius Hemphill big band in 1988 [*Hines Interview*].[183]

David Hines, late 1980s. *Photograph by Roscoe Crenshaw, with permission from Joyce Byers Hines.*

The renaissance of jazz in St. Louis really began when Barbara Rose (later known affectionately by musicians as the "Jazz Mom") tried to initiate a jazz party in the late 1980s. This event never happened, because St. Louis is a "walk-up" town when it comes to entertainment. People apparently didn't like having to put up money six months in advance. Undaunted, she found a room in the Hotel Majestic in late 1990 and opened a "listening room" jazz club, Just Jazz, which became a big success. When the Majestic was sold, Barbara moved her operation to the Bistro in Grand Center and named her organization Jazz at the Bistro. She did an important thing: she took Jazz at the Bistro to nonprofit status and successfully ran the club until her death in 1998. Just Jazz was unusual in that the bandstand was in a corner facing the bar with seating going in both directions along what felt like narrow halls. Both local and an amazing number of national musicians were heard at both venues. Barbara knew the value of publicity, and the club seemed to be packed with every engagement. The *Post-Dispatch* had 160 mentions of Just Jazz in the years 1990 to 1995. This investment in the music by Barbara Rose led directly to the organization Jazz St. Louis (second incarnation), its continuing success and the completion of one of the best jazz clubs in the world, the Ferring Jazz Bistro.

A STABLE JAZZ SCENE (1996–2008)

W e have discussed the effect of the technological shift of talking pictures on the employment of musicians in St. Louis in the 1920s. Another technological shift took place in the late 1980s, when digital technology replaced phonographs playing spinning discs with the sound being decoded by "needles." The average two-sided LP held about forty-five minutes of music and was made of vinyl. The CD is a disc made of space-age plastic that is read and decoded by a laser beam and can hold up to eighty minutes of music. Digital technology also made recording easier and much cheaper. This resulted in a glut of CDs. It also brought about a reissue mania, so that all the great (and not so great) recordings of the past could be repackaged and sold again.

This period was marked politically by the "Gingrich Revolution" (1994), which made the political class increasingly polarized and out of touch with regular citizens. The Al-Qaeda attacks on September 11, 2001, led to more fear, tribalism and loss of civil liberties that is still increasing. The "War on Drugs" continued to imprison more of our minority citizens. It appears that the jazz scene in St. Louis came through these events and the "Dot-Com Bubble" (1995–2000) stronger than ever.

The Australian pianist Simon Rowe started Catalyst Records in 1997. Rowe then moved to Indiana, taking the label with him in 2000. Bill Becker started the Victoria Company in 1997 in St. Louis and soon became involved with Greg Trampe's MusicMasters studio, which recorded half the CDs and manufactured them all. This label is responsible for many of the recordings of our musicians up to today. We owe him a debt of gratitude for his work documenting St. Louis jazz musicians.

Rich McDonnell started MaxJazz, a label that initially featured jazz vocalists but soon branched out. The label was active until his death in 2014. Its catalog has since been bought by Mack Avenue Records. Jay Zelinka started Freedonia Music to record, preserve and reissue free St. Louis improvisation from the 1970s and 1980s. Mike and Rob Silverman started Autumn Hill Records in 2007. The company produces both jazz and "new age" music.

In addition to the *Post-Dispatch*, the *American* and the *Argus*, jazz in this period and up to today got more media help in 2005 with the pianist Dean Minderman's *St. Louis Jazz Notes* blog. Reviews of local musicians' performances were rare in all of the media.

After Barbara Rose's death in 1998, Gene Dobbs Bradford became the director of Jazz at the Bistro in early 2000. The club became even more of a success and continues as one of the best jazz clubs in the world [*Bradford Interview*]. Its educational programs are described in chapter 10. During this time, seven recordings were made at the facility: three by Ralph Sutton (1999–2000) and one each by Peter Martin (2001), Bennie Green and Russell Malone (2002), Kim Massie (2005) and Lamar Harris (2008).

The Sheldon Concert Hall started a jazz series in 1996, bringing in four or five national musicians and groups during its season. Since 2004, vocalist Denise Thimes has presented an annual concert at the Sheldon honoring her mother and raising money for the Mildred Thimes Foundation to fight pancreatic cancer. The Sheldon also has a Notes from Home Concert Series that showcases local musicians. There is also a series of "coffee concerts" at 10:00 a.m. featuring local musicians that appeals to older listeners.

The Webster University Jazz Series during the school year presents local musicians and students on Monday nights at the Winifred Moore Auditorium. The author remembers a memorable concert by its big band, playing the music of Charles Mingus—it seemed the spirit of Mingus was present in the building and took over the band. The students played way over their heads in a rage that reflected the Mingus personality. Washington University's Jazz at Holmes regularly presents both local and some national jazz musicians. Drummer Maurice Carnes's Hip Jazz Quintet recorded there in 2004 [*Discography*]. Both series continue today.

Mississippi Nights and BB's Jazz, Blues and Soups present local and national touring jazz musicians occasionally. The Delmar Loop had several restaurants that feature local musicians. For years, the Sessions Big Band

Chapter 9

St. Louis Stompers at the Whitaker Jazz Festival, Shaw's Garden, 2006. *Photograph by Dennis Owsley, with permission from Steve Lilley.*

played at BB's Jazz Blues and Soups on an every-Monday basis. The Whitaker Jazz Series has been running in the late spring at the Missouri Botanical Garden for years. As the years have gone by, other music has supplanted some of the jazz. In Webster Groves, Crossings Tavern and Grille and Cookie's Jazz & More opened at about the same time and closed at about the same time (2008).

Contemporary Productions' Steve Schankman opened the Finale, which advertised fine dining and jazz in Clayton. The club opened in March 2005 and closed at the end of 2007, when the club lost its lease. It never reopened, but it had a fine lineup of national musicians and local musicians until it closed.

In 2002, jazz radio personality Don Wolff and his wife established the Don and Heidi Wolff Jazz Institute and Art Gallery at Harris-Stowe State University.[184] This is a huge repository of recordings from Wolff's collection. It also encompasses other musical genres. It has listening booths, recorded interviews and a lot of memorabilia. There is also a Jazz Hall of Fame.

Trumpeter George Sams grew up in St. Louis and, while in high school, hung out with people like Julius Hemphill, Oliver Lake and Bobby Danzig. He worked in East St. Louis blues clubs. He moved to San Francisco at age nineteen and worked with forward-thinking musicians such as Jon Jang and Andrew Hill. His group United Front was recorded in Berlin in 1982.[185] During most of his career, Sams has been involved with arts organizations. He returned to St. Louis in the late 1980s and founded the Metropolitan Gallery on Locust in 2005. The gallery closed in 2014. He also established the Nu-Art series, which featured concerts by local and national musicians at a variety of venues. That series continues today with a YouTube archive of more than one hundred videos of Nu-Art series concerts.[186]

Dixieland continued to be a staple of St. Louis jazz, and two long-lived bands, the St. Louis Stompers and Cornet Chop Suey, were founded during this time. The St. Louis Jazz Club presented monthly concerts and had an annual picnic, a practice that continues today. The Mid-America Jazz Festival continued to have Dixieland and mainstream jazz up to 1999. Victor Voland profiled Charlie Wells, the founder and promoter of the festival, in the *Post-Dispatch* (June 12, 2001). Wells died in 2002.

Between 1996 and 2008, there were 142 recordings (10.9 per year) by musicians who live and work in the Greater St. Louis area; 37 (26.1 percent) of them were either Dixieland or ragtime. Even though two new bands started, the age of the St. Louis Jazz Club members was a concern. It seems the *Post-Dispatch* had as many obituaries of its members as there were Jazz Club mentions.

Pianist and vocalist Jean Kittrell led three ensembles: the Jazz Incredibles (a trio), the seven-piece St. Louis Rivermen and the five-piece Old St. Louis Levee Band. The Rivermen made nine recordings in this period, the Jazz Incredibles made three and the Old St. Louis Levee Band made one recording [*Discography*]. She was also heard in a duet with bassist Jay Hungerford on his CD *Keys to the City* (1995) [*Discography*]. She retired in 2008 and died in 2018. The musicians in these groups were: Jean Kittrell (piano, vocal), Glenn Meyer or Noel Katalesky (clarinet), Brett Stamps or the late Pat Arana (trombone), Steve Lilley (cornet), John Becker or Bobbie Grimm (banjo), David "Red" Lehr (sousaphone) and Don Schroeder or Rick Schaumberger (drums). After Kittrell retired, Red Lehr took over the Rivermen and started his own group, the Powerhouse Five.

The personnel of the St. Louis Stompers Classic Jazz Band, one of the newer bands, has been drawn from these musicians: Joe Thompson (trumpet), Jack Tartar (drums), Jeff Chronister or Don Franz (tuba), Joe Schulte (trombone and tuba), Steve Lilley (cornet), Bobby Grimm (banjo), Dave Majchrzak (piano) and Mike Lilley (clarinet, soprano saxophone). Between 1998 and 2018, the band recorded eleven titles [*Discography*].

Jean Kittrell and the St. Louis Rivermen, 2006. © *SIUE Library and Information Services, with permission from Jean Kittrell.*

Another long-lived Dixieland/Show band, Cornet Chop Suey, was organized in 2000 and is still working and recording. In the 2000–08 period, they made a total of six recordings with the following personnel: Al Sherman (bass, electric bass), Jerry Epperson (reeds), Tommy Tucker (cornet, vocal), John Gillick (drums), Bob Row (piano, vocal) or Paul Reid (piano), Jimmy Haislip or Brett Stamps (trombone) and Brian Casserly (trumpet, vocal) [*Discography*].

The St. Louis Ragtimers recorded in 2001, while their pianist, Trebor Tichenor, made two recordings. Pianist Richard Egan made two ragtime recordings (2000, 2004). Another ragtime and stride pianist, a young Stephanie Trick, also recorded twice (2005, 2008) [*Discography*]. Trick[187] now lives half the year in Italy with her husband, Paolo Alderighi, who is also a pianist. They tour the world together.

Trebor Tichenor is a St. Louis–born ragtime pianist and scholar. If it weren't for his efforts in preserving and making ragtime a living music since 1960, ragtime in St. Louis might have been forgotten like other parts of our history. He began performing on Gaslight Square in 1961. He was the author of many articles and, with David Jasen, published the book *Rags and Ragtime* in 1978.

He was also a composer of ragtime music and a lecturer in music at Washington University, teaching the ragtime class. Tichenor died on February 22, 2014, at the age of seventy-four. His two children, Virginia and Andrew, are both professional musicians.

Although St. Louis is regarded as a trumpet player's town, a good argument can be made that it is also a piano player's town. The reason is that piano players (and guitar players as well) can work steadily in hotel entertainment rooms, restaurants, piano bars and other venues. According to the number of mentions in the *Post-Dispatch* during this time, Herb Drury, Carolbeth True, Dave Venn, Ptah Williams, Kim Portnoy, Reggie Thomas, Carol Schmidt, Curt Landes, Eddie Fritz and others had as much work as they wanted. Quite a few made recordings [*Discography*].

Pianist Ptah Williams is a wizard. He has been around St. Louis since the late 1970s and has worked continuously since then. Ptah played with Lou Donaldson and Fontella Bass. He and bassist Darryl Mixon toured Europe with drummer Ed Thigpen in the 1980s. Ptah, Darryl and drummer Gary Sykes formed the group Tracer in the mid-1980s, and it has been a St. Louis favorite, reuniting occasionally.

In 2004, Carolbeth True received the *St. Louis Magazine* Musician of the Year Award in addition to the American Federation of Musicians Local 2-197 Owen Miller Award for service and dedication. She and her trio made a CD with harmonica player Sandy Weltman in 1997. Her working group is now Two Times True with her son David True on drums [*True Interview* and *Discography*].

Top: Ptah Williams. *Courtesy Mike Silverman, with permission from Ptah Williams.*

Bottom: Darryl Mixon, 1987. *Photograph by Dennis Owsley, with permission from Darryl Mixon.*

Herb Drury and Jerry Cherry recorded three CDs during this period. Dave Venn and Herb recorded piano duets for Bill Becker's Victoria Company label in 1996. Becker's label has a catalog of over sixty releases, mainly mainstream jazz, most featuring St. Louis artists. Venn recorded an album of solo, duo and trio music for Becker in 1997 [*Discography*].

Kim Portnoy[188] is a Herb Drury piano student and Washington University graduate. He has been part of the Webster University jazz faculty for years. Kim is an imaginative composer of both jazz and classical music. He works and has recorded with his own trio and occasionally presents big band concerts of his compositions and arrangements. His big band was recorded in 1997 and featured Linda Pressgrave's French horn as part of the brass section [*Discography*].

Eddie Fritz remained very busy in piano venues like the Breckenridge Hotel in Frontenac, the Chase Park Plaza and the Ritz-Carlton. He was profiled in a 1998 article in the *Post-Dispatch*. Fritz died in 2012.

Pianist Ray Kennedy, even though he lived in New York, returned to St. Louis and made seven recordings from 1996 to 2005, often in the company of his bassist brother, Tom. Ray was recorded on Tom Kennedy's 1996 CD and as part of a trio (1997); with vocalist-pianist Christine Hitt (1997 and 1998); with Asa Harris (1999); in an all-star group with Willie Akins, Scott Alberici and others (2000); with vocalist Sherry Drake (2004); and in a quartet with guitarist Howard Alden (2005) [*Discography*].

Lawrence Fields, who was born in St. Louis and is a 2008 graduate of the Berklee College of Music, initially worked with Willie Akins and recorded with Maurice Carnes and John Norment [*Discography*]. Since leaving Berklee, Fields has played with many of the greatest musicians in jazz.[189]

Pianist Jeter Thompson made three recordings during this period. The first was a quintet with Freddie Washington (reeds), Ben Jones (trumpet) and his brothers Harold (bass) and Howard (drums) sometime around 2000. The second was a trio with his brothers (2005), and the third was with his niece Danita Mumphard (2005), recorded at Cookie's Jazz & More in Webster Groves (2005) [*Discography*]. Jeter worked as a cartographer for the Defense Mapping Agency in St. Louis. He died on December 1, 2017.

Guitarists also worked a lot during this period. Steve Schenkel and Dan Rubright were recorded three times using folk songs and religious material (1998, 2001 and 2002). Schenkel also recorded with pianist Dave Venn and vocalists Debby Lennon and Ashley Mason [*Discography*].

Steve Schenkel has brought more than jazz guitar to St. Louis. A graduate of SIU-Edwardsville, he also earned a PhD in music from Washington

Dave Black, 2004. *Photograph by Dennis Owsley, with permission from Dave Black.*

University and an MA in religion from Webster University. He founded the Webster Jazz Studies Program in 1980 and, until his retirement, taught music, media and religion. His compositions are heard on PBS, at the Gateway Arch and at other venues in St. Louis. He plays with the St. Louis Symphony and in the Fox Theater Orchestra. Schenkel retired from Webster University in 2018.[190]

Guitarist Rob Block taught at Webster University for ten years and recorded with vocalist Michele Shaheen (1994) and Dave Venn (2006). He moved to New Orleans to work with his brother Dan and then moved to New York.[191] Dave Black plays guitar in both folk and jazz settings in many venues throughout the St. Louis area. He recorded with Brilliant Corners (1997), on Sandy Weltman and Carolbeth True's New World Harmonica Jazz recording (1998), with Fred Tompkins (1999 and 2001) and led his own recording in 2000.[192]

Tom Byrne[193] plays guitar in a number of situations and today seems to be working nearly every night in restaurants and clubs. He recorded with the Portnoy Big Band (1997), with Reggie and Mardra Thomas (1998), with vocalist Valerie Tichacek (2003) and made his own recording that same year [*Discography*].

Rick Haydon recorded with Brett Stamps, Jim Owens, Reggie and Mardra Thomas, John Pizzarelli, Asa Harris and Christine Hitt. Haydon teaches at Southern Illinois–Edwardsville.[194] Guitarist William Linehan[195] is a senior

Reggie and Mardra Thomas. *Courtesy Reggie and Mardra Thomas, with permission.*

lecturer in the music department of Washington University and teaches the jazz theory and performance courses. He lives part of the year in Italy.

Swing DeVille is a band dedicated to the style of the Hot Club of France and Django Reinhardt. They recorded in 2006. The band has all string instruments. Another band that is unusual is Bach to the Future. It fuses Bach with a jazz-rock style. The Silverman brothers started the band, which was recorded in 2006 [*Discography*].

Willem von Hombracht[196] teaches bass at Webster University. He plays with the faculty jazz ensemble and has performed in many musical styles and also directs master classes and workshops in the United States and in Europe. Willem is on the faculty of the International Summer Jazz Academy

Bach to the Future, 2006.
Photographer unknown. Courtesy Mike and Rob Silverman.

in Poland and was named artistic director in 2008. Bassist Jon Thomas, who worked mainly in the Delmar Loop, recorded two CDs in 2001 and 2002 [*Discography*]. Other bassists active in this time are Ben Wheeler, Bob DeBoo, Zeb Briskovich (Southern Illinois University) and Ric Vice, a retired elementary school librarian.

Community radio station **KDHX** had a long-running jazz vocal show hosted by Al Becker called *Voices in the Night*. The show finally ended in 2010.

Vocalist Denise Thimes,[197] daughter of St. Louis radio personality Lou "Fatha" Thimes, has worked in the city since 1987. In addition to her powerful voice, Denise is an actress, appearing in Black Repertory Theater and St. Louis Repertory Theater productions. She has toured all over the world, sung with many jazz greats and, in 2018, moved to Chicago to further her career. Her recordings can be found in the *Discography*.

Jeanne Trevor, always a St. Louis vocal favorite, continued working through this period. She made a 1999 recording for Catalyst Productions featuring Willie Akins on tenor saxophone. Lester Bowie's first wife, Fontella Bass, made a recording with vocalists Tracey Mitchell (also guitar) and Marsha Evans in 2000 [*Discography*].

Pianist-vocalist Christine Hitt was on the Webster University faculty and worked in St. Louis in this period. She recorded a 1997 CD for MaxJazz. Her husband is in the military, and they moved to Nebraska at the end of the decade. Asa Harris, whose career was covered in chapter 8, recorded for MaxJazz in 1999 [*both Discography*].

Denise Thimes. *Photographer unknown. Courtesy Denise Thimes.*

Vocalist Mae Wheeler ("Lady Jazz")[198] subbed for Jeanne Trevor on Gaslight Square, according to John Becker.[199] From Memphis, she began singing in church at age four. She was recorded in concert in 2001. Interestingly enough, her coverage in the *Post-Dispatch* was very minimal until the late 1980s. Throughout her career, she always promoted younger local singers by showcasing them on her "Divas" concerts at Westport Playhouse and at the Sheldon Concert Hall. Mae died in 2011.

Minnesota native Erin Bode is a graduate of the Webster University Jazz program. That program encourages its students to perform in the community [*Bode Interview*]. She made her first recording (self-produced) in 2001. This gave an entrée into MaxJazz, for whom she recorded two CDs that put her on the map nationally and internationally [*Discography*]. While she lives and performs in St. Louis with her husband, bassist Sid Rodway, all of her recordings after 2001 have been made in other locales. She continues to perform around the world.

Vocalist Valerie Tichacek[200] won the *Downbeat* "Outstanding Performance by a Collegiate Jazz Vocalist" award in 2002. Valerie made a 2003 recording. She hosted and coproduced a YouTube show, *Jazz at Cookies*, has her own trio and sings with the Original Knights of Swing Big Band. Sherry Drake

Left: Erin Bode. *Courtesy Erin Bode, with permission.*

Below: Reggie Thomas OGD Trio. © *Reggie Thomas, with permissions from Reggie Thomas, Rick Haydon and Miles Vandiver.*

has sung in St. Louis for many years. She made her only recording in 2004 [*both Discography*].

Born in St. Louis, versatile vocalist-keyboardist Anita Rosamond returned to the city and made two recordings in 2006 and one in 2008. She is still very active today, as is Ellen Martinez, who recorded in 2007 [*Discography*].

Vocalist Mardra Thomas and her husband, pianist-organist Reggie Thomas, worked in St. Louis and around the Midwest during this period. They made two recordings (1998, 2005) [*Discography*]. Reggie also led a group called OGD (organ, guitar, drums) with Rick Haydon (guitar) and Miles Vandiver (drums). Mardra is also a versatile actress, starring in award-winning productions of *Lady Day at Emerson Bar & Grille* and *Lady Day at the Boston Bistro*. They now live in DeKalb, Illinois.[201]

World-class vocalist Debby Lennon[202] grew up in Webster Groves and studied at Fontbonne College. She spent eight years with the a cappella jazz vocal ensemble Pieces of Eight. She is also an actress and opera singer, working in many theaters in St. Louis, and is a member of the St. Louis Symphony chorus. Debby teaches voice at Webster University and directs the jazz choir. She made her first recording as a leader in 2005 and has appeared on several other recordings that will be detailed in chapter 10 [*Discography*].

Pianist-vocalist Hugh "Peanuts" Whalum worked steadily in this period. His Nat "King" Cole–style voice was very popular. He made his first, well-received recording as a leader in 2006 at the age of seventy-five [*Discography*].

Organist Terry Williams has been working in St. Louis since the late 1950s and has played with Gene Ammons, Sonny Stitt and other name musicians. Pianist Jimmy Jones has been around town for many years and is the coauthor of a book with Lynne Driggs Cunningham on St. Louis musicians.[203] He and Williams recorded a CD together in 2004 [*Discography*].

Trumpeter-pianist Lee Hyde put together a band that he called his "Gentle Jazz" group, reminiscent of the 1959 Jazz Central group. They recorded in 1998 [*Discography*]. Other St. Louis trumpeters include Randall Holmes, who was on the Webster faculty and led his Hard Bop Heritage

Debby Lennon, 2003. *Photograph by Dennis Owsley, with permission from Debby Lennon.*

Randall Holmes, 2003. *Photograph by Dennis Owsley, with permission from Randall Holmes.*

Quintet in two recordings (one issued, 2008). Danny Campbell recorded with trumpeter-composer Prince Wells (2002). We have covered Jim Manley's big band work. Larry Wilson, a trumpeter from East St. Louis, recorded in 1996 and 1998.

Trumpeter Michael Parkinson[204] served as music department chair at Webster University (1997–2007). Parkinson performed with the Webster Faculty Jazz Ensemble and the Paul DeMarinis Quartet. He, along with Dr. Barrett Babler, started the certificate in entrepreneurship/music. He started the New Music Ensemble and the Mini Big Band, which did not work from music paper. He has had a distinguished career and is now the director of the School of Music at Middle Tennessee State University.

Composer-trumpeter Prince Wells[205] started the Black Music Society of Missouri around 1985 and has worked with many groups, including the Jazz

Michael Parkinson, 2003. *Photograph by Dennis Owsley, with permission from Michael Parkinson.*

Edge Big Band. He joined the Southern Illinois University–Edwardsville music department in 1989 and is now the director of the music business program. He recorded a CD of his compositions in 2002 [*Discography*].

On December 26, 1996, the *Post-Dispatch* highlighted the Young Jazz Messengers, a group of high school students with uncommon talents. Keyon Harrold (trumpet) was from McCluer High School; Jason Salter (sax) was from Chaminade. The others, from Central Visual and Performing Arts High School, were Corey James (piano), Jason Jennings (vibes), Jahmal Nichols (bass) and Jeremy Clemons (drums). Terry Perkins commented, "Harrold has a natural touch on trumpet you just can't teach." Clemons[206] now lives and works in New York.

Harrold[207] went to New York and has played with Wynton Marsalis, Christian McBride, the Count Basie ghost band, the Charles Tolliver Big Band and others too numerous to mention. He graduated from the School of Jazz at the New School and has also been active in the rhythm and blues and hip-hop worlds. Keyon did the entire trumpet playing in Don Cheadle's *Kind of Blue*, a biopic of Miles Davis. The *All-Music Guide* singled him out as one of "the leading jazz trumpet players of a new generation."

Trombonist Brett Stamps[208] was the founder and director (1979) of the jazz studies program at Southern Illinois University–Edwardsville, retiring from that position in 2011. He played with Stan Kenton, the U.S. Army Jazz Ambassadors and Jean Kittrell. He now plays with Cornet Chop

Keyon Harrold. *Photographer unknown. Courtesy Keyon Harrold, with permission.*

Suey. Two other trombonists, Jim Owens and Lamar Harris, recorded in this period [*Discography*].

James Martin[209] is a jazz and classical trombonist and bass trombonist who was born in St. Louis. He was a member of the Buddy Rich band (1988–89) and moved back to St. Louis in 1990. He has played and recorded with the St. Louis Symphony and performs in the orchestra pits of the Fox Theater and Muny Opera. He also plays in the St. Louis Brass Ensemble.

Trombonist Jim Owens[210] is a graduate of both Southern Illinois University campuses. He is a freelance player who performs and has recorded with many of St. Louis's big bands. In 2015, Jim became the music director of the Gateway City Big Band.

Clarinetist Scott Alberici plays in both Dixieland and mainstream jazz bands. During this period, he recorded with Reggie and Mardra Thomas, Christine Hitt, Sherry Drake, Ray Kennedy and the Steve Schenkel–Dan Rubright duo [*Discography*]. He is still active today.

Paul DeMarinis,[211] now director of the jazz department at Webster University, has been a force in the music since the late 1970s. A University City High School and Indiana University graduate, he is a composer, author, poet (see chapter 10) and saxophone player for the St. Louis Symphony. He was also a faculty member for the Jamey Aebersold jazz camps. During this period, he made two recordings, one issued (1997). His group, Brilliant Corners, featured Dave Black (guitar), Dan Eubanks (bass) and Kevin Gianino (drums) [*Discography*].

Tenor saxophonist Willie Akins recorded for Catalyst Productions in 1998 and became part of the Webster University faculty during this period [*Discography*]. Willie made one more recording (see chapter 10) before he died in 2015.

Saxophonist Mike Karpowitz is a graduate of Southern Illinois University and is a member of the Webster University faculty. He has a large résumé in theater music, commercial music and jazz. Mike is also director of bands at DeSmet High School.

Baritone saxophonist Dr. Rob Hughes is a music professor at St. Louis University. He has worked with the Kim Portnoy Big Band and others. His PhD dissertation from Washington University is "Howard Rumsey's Lighthouse All-Stars: Modern Jazz in California, 1948–1959."

Dave Stone continued his career and became associated with Jay Zelinka's free jazz efforts. In 1996, he started a twenty-two-year residency at Manga Italiano that continues today. Stone recorded a CD of solo saxophone in 1998. This was among a cluster of five CDs reissued by Freedonia in 1997–99 with Zelinka, Mills and others. Two more CDs were recorded in 2008 and 2009 [*Discography*].

The Bosman twins, Dwayne and Dwight, mainly played private events, taught school and had two gigs a year at BB's Jazz, Blues and Soups during this time.

Composer Fred Tompkins[212] recorded three CDs during this period and was associated with the New Music Circle, which presents avant-garde music played by many local and national jazz musicians [*Discography*].

Top, left: Willie Akins, 2004. *Photograph by Dennis Owsley, with permission from Sandy Akins.*

Top, right: Scott Alberici, 2010. *Photograph by Dennis Owsley, with permission from Scott Alberici.*

Bottom: Paul DeMarinis, 2005. *Photograph by Dennis Owsley, with permission from Paul DeMarinis.*

Soprano, alto and tenor saxophonist John Norment was born in St. Louis in 1942. He worked on cruise ships for several years and in just about every venue that presented jazz in St. Louis. The *Riverfront Times* named him "Best Jazz Artist" in 2003. His playing also encompassed church music. He made one recording, issued posthumously in 2007 [*Discography*]. Norment died in 2005.[213]

Alto saxophonist Jason Swagler spent this period working as a sideman for many bands, including those of Keith Ellis, Jim Manley and vocalist Suzie Thorne. The rest of his career will be detailed in chapter 10. Saxophonist Larry Johnson makes his living playing rock 'n' roll but has recorded with Jim Manley, Brett Spainhower and as part of Carolbeth True's Two Times True group. Chapter 10 will bring his career up to date. Tenor saxophonist–bassist Jeff Anderson recorded with Mae Wheeler (2001) and Prince Wells (2002) as a bassist [*Discography*]. Tenor saxophonist Larry Smith works with Randall Holmes Hard Bop Heritage group and during this period recorded with Holmes, Keith Ellis, Brett Spainhower and Jim Manley [*all Discography*].

St. Louis has three tenor saxophonists working in the smooth jazz genre: Rodney Tate, James Warfield and Tim Cunningham. Cunningham made a total of five recordings in this period. Warfield also recorded with Keith Ellis [*all Discography*].

Drummer Kevin Gianino[214] is a Webster faculty member and has served as a faculty member for the International Summer Jazz Academy in Poland, the Webster Summer Jazz Combo Camp and the Jim Widner Summer Jazz Camps. He has played with just about everybody in St. Louis.

Drummer Kimberley Thompson[215] was born in Los Angeles but raised in St. Louis. A graduate of Pattonville High School, she worked with Willie Akins and others. She graduated from the Manhattan School of Music in 2003 and plays with pop and jazz greats, garnering three Grammy awards. She has also won awards for her compositions.

Maurice Carnes is a first-call drummer who has toured Europe and Asia with Marcus Roberts.[216] He lives in St. Louis. His hip jazz quintet was recorded at Holmes Lounge in 2004 [*Discography*]. Clancy Newell plays in several big bands around St. Louis and is a member of the Kim Portnoy Trio.

Drummer Tommy Crane[217] played in St. Louis with Willie Akins and moved to New York, where he leads a jazz-rock fusion band. In 2006, he toured with the Mingus Big Band. Jim Orso[218] worked with Paul DeMarinis and Dave Stone in St. Louis. He is now a rock drummer in New York.

Emmanuel Harrold[219] is Keyon Harrold's brother. He went to McCluer High School and was a professional at seventeen. In St. Louis, he was part of

Kevin Gianino, 2004. *Photograph by Dennis Owsley, with permission from Kevin Gianino.*

Willie Akins's quartet. He earned his MFA at the New School University in New York in 2008 and has played and recorded with many jazz and hip-hop musicians. He has several Grammy awards to his credit.

Drummers Kyle Honeycutt and Gary Sykes have been heard in many contexts from jazz-rock to avant-garde and are still active today.

Miles Vandiver[220] has played drums for many local and national artists. He is drum-set instructor and coordinator of recording activities for Southern Illinois University–Edwardsville.

In this period, there were four festivals in the spring. All highlighted local artists, but the US Bank Festival brought in many national groups. Cynthia Prost was the festival founder and director. It was held in Clayton's Shaw Park (2001–08). Soon, it was apparent that one of the unstated goals of the festival was racial diversity, missing the data that the black community has moved on and now likes jazz at about the same rate as the white community.[221] To get to this diversity, the festival started bringing in soul singers and other non-jazz acts. It became a jazz and heritage festival. St. Louis's very hot, stormy June weather caused the cancelation of several performances and the entire festival in 2008. In contrast, the Greater St. Louis Jazz Festival is held indoors at the University of Missouri–St. Louis and at Jazz at the Bistro. The festival features local musicians, high school bands and one or more headliners. The Old Webster Jazz & Blues Festival started in 2002 in October with mainly Dixieland bands. As time went on, more mainstream jazz and blues acts were heard.

The storms that brought down the US Bank Festival are symbolic of the economic storm that fell on St. Louis with the coming of the Great Recession that started in late 2008 and lasted until 2010.

Chapter 10

SLOW RECOVERY FROM THE GREAT RECESSION OF 2008

As a result of massive and risky real estate speculation and other economic problems, the late fall of 2008 was the beginning of what is known today as the "Great Recession." A look at the *Discography* shows evidence of the massive downturn that hit the country and the St. Louis jazz community. In the years 1996–2008, jazz recording activity averaged 10.9 CDs per year; in 2009–18, that average was 7.9 CDs or all-digital recordings per year. Reflecting the aging of the St. Louis Jazz Club members, the average number of new Dixieland-ragtime recordings per year fell by more than two-thirds, but the St. Louis Jazz Club continues its monthly meetings and concerts.

The Finale closed, and the US Bank Jazz Festival in Clayton ended in 2008, but Jazz St. Louis continued to prosper. It built a magnificent new facility by acquiring the building next to the Bistro and converting it into the Harold and Dorothy Steward Center for Jazz, an edifice with the Ferring Jazz Bistro, practice rooms for the jazz students and Nancy's Lounge, a room where patrons can watch the shows without charge. Since 2000, over 160,000 students—60 percent of whom are from low-income communities—have been touched by the organization's jazz education wing. Currently, Jazz St. Louis offers six programs.[222]

- *Jazz U puts middle and high school students in small jazz combos that meet during the year.*
- *Webop is an early-childhood program for children three to five years old with their families.*

- *Emerson Jazz in the Schools puts students from St. Louis–area schools in contact with world-class musicians both at the Bistro and in the schools.*
- *Jazz Academy is for middle school students wanting to perform music and improve their instrumental technique. It meets weekly.*
- *There are residencies by world-class musicians and educators who travel in the area conducting master classes and clinics.*
- *Elementary Curriculum Partnerships is a district-wide initiative that focuses on bringing the deeper concepts of jazz music to general music teachers.*

Nationally known groups the Wee Three Trio and trumpeter Sean Jones were recorded at the Bistro in 2013 and 2015, respectively [*Discography*].

A major problem in the region is the racial divide and mistrust among the white community, the police and minority communities. This has come to a head twice. The Michael Brown shooting on August 9, 2014, sparked riots, and the lack of transparency on the part of the prosecutor, state government and police fueled this mistrust. Similar reactions occurred for the same reasons with the verdict in the Jason Shockley case on September 16, 2017.

Ferring Jazz Bistro. © *Jazz St. Louis, with permission.*

The experiences of all races with Jazz St. Louis's programs are among the few shining lights that can help this divide.

The jazz series at the Sheldon Concert Hall and the Touhill Performing Arts Center continued during this period. BB's Jazz, Blues and Soups, the Broadway Oyster Bar, the Delmar Loop in University City, the Whitaker Series at the Missouri Botanical Garden, the Webster University Jazz Series and the Holmes Lounge at Washington University all offered places for local musicians to play. Even at the height of the recession, there were a number of places where jazz could be heard. Robbie's House of Jazz in Webster Groves (2009–14), the Wine Press (now closed), Nathalie's, Troy's Jazz Gallery, the Thurman Grill, the Kinda Blue Club and the Cigar Inn in Belleville are still available to jazz fans. The Tavern of the Fine Arts on Bell Avenue in St. Louis (2011–16) was a place for more advanced playing. The Kreuzberg Center has three spaces where jazz is heard: the Kranzberg Center (weekly jam sessions); the Grandel Theater; and, inside the Grandel, a jazz room, the Dark Room. Hotel entertainment rooms also provide work for local musicians. Dan Stevens renovated the Ozark Theater in Webster and turned it into a jazz concert hall. It continues as the Webster Groves Concert Hall. At least one concert a month is devoted to jazz. But, because of the recession, the number of gigs was down, at least until early 2011.

Jazz radio was, at one time, the place to go for information on places in the community to hear jazz. WSIE, formerly a full-time jazz station, has fallen on hard times. Hopefully, the station will come back with new management. At present, the author's show, *Jazz Unlimited*, on St. Louis Public Radio, and Josh Weinstein's *All Soul, No Borders* on KDHX may be the only locally produced jazz-themed shows in St. Louis. Currently, WSIE's programming is a mix of jazz, smooth jazz, blues and soft rock. Smooth jazz stations came and went during this period.

The *Post-Dispatch* was sold in 2005 to Lee Enterprises of Iowa.[223] Jobs and circulation have dropped in the years since the sale. Even with the paper's online edition, reviews and previews of jazz performances are nearly nonexistent. Around 2008, the publicity for Webster University jazz concerts stopped, and audience numbers have fallen. Dean Minderman's *St. Louis Jazz Notes* blog continues to inform the community about what is going on in jazz.

The Greater St. Louis Jazz Festival, the University City Jazz Festival (started 2012), the Chesterfield Jazz Festival (started 2013) and the Old Webster Jazz and Blues Festival continue. The latter three are free and outside in the early spring and fall.

People who are nostalgic for a certain type of big band music often ask the question, "Will the big bands ever come back?" The big bands that they hunger for are the swing bands of their youth, which are out of fashion and can never return to their previous glory. The answer is that big bands and their style of jazz evolved with the times. It can safely be said that there are more big bands heard today than at the height of the swing era. With few exceptions, they are local big bands. Big bands always trained young musicians to read, phrase and interpret music beyond the lead sheets that are used in combos. That learning experience has morphed into a progression of junior high school, high school and college big bands. Nearly every high school and college or university with a music department has at least one big band.[224]

Local big bands play in towns and cities everywhere in the country. In the major cities, the top bands are staffed professionals working full-time as studio musicians, in clubs or in symphony orchestras. "Community big bands" are big bands staffed by music teachers, other working musicians and people who work in other professions. The common purpose is for the players to have fun and sharpen their skills by enjoying the challenge of reading and interpreting big band music. These community big bands play music in every style, from the dance music of the big band era to quite modern music.

St. Louis has several community big bands. The Gateway City Big Band has been in existence since 1966 and is morphing into a jazz band. The Blue Knights is a smaller band that is an offshoot of the Gateway City Big Band. The original Knights of Swing band was founded in 1950 in Minnesota and remains active today. The Ambassadors of Swing also mines this area. The Oasis big band rehearses and plays occasional concerts.

The Sessions Big Band was started around 1995 by Keith Ellis as a band to play Monday nights at BB's Jazz, Blues and Soups. Ellis died in 1999, but the band continues. The music is jazz classics and jazz standards composed since the mid-1950s. It now continues on a monthly basis. There is a St. Louis Big Band, the Steve Schankman Orchestra, the Dave Dickey Big Band, the Genesis Jazz Project, the Route 66 Big Band, the Missouri Bottom Big Band and the North County Big Band (a high school all-star band). Another long-standing band, the Jazz Edge Orchestra, was formed in January 1990 under the direction of Robert Edwards. This band has a Count Basie feel to it.

From Lebanon, Missouri, bassist Jim Widner played with Stan Kenton and Woody Herman. He is now director of jazz studies at the University of

Missouri–St. Louis. He runs an annual jazz summer camp at the university. Although he is primarily a teacher, he also leads his own St. Louis Big Band [*Widner Interview*] that was recorded in 2013 [*Discography*].

The Gateway City Big Band has made eight recordings, and the Ambassadors of Swing made one recording. Keith Ellis and the Sessions Big Band recorded two CDs in 1999. Trumpeter Jim Manley led studio orchestras in five recordings (2001 to 2011) in a style related to the Maynard Ferguson band. The Kim Portnoy Big Band, which performs irregularly, recorded a CD in 1997 [*all Discography*]. Trumpeter Gary Dammer lives on the East Side and was in the U.S. Air Force Band for many years. He led a big band that recorded at the Florissant Community Center in 2005.

Since the retirement of Jean Kittrell, sousaphonist David "Red" Lehr has taken over leadership of the St. Louis Rivermen; started his group, the Powerhouse Five, with the same instrumentation of her Old St. Louis Levee Band; and retired the Jazz Incredibles concept. He made two recordings in this period. The St. Louis Stompers and its pianist, Dr. Dave Majchrzak, issued five recordings. Cornet Chop Suey made three recordings, and Stephanie Trick made two recordings, one live at the Sheldon. Richard Egan made the only other ragtime recording in this period [*all Discography*].

Drummer Steve Davis[225] (born 1958) was born in Santa Barbara, California. Shelly Manne was his godfather. He is an educator, sound engineer and producer while being one of the most innovative drummers in jazz. He toured with the Lynne Arriale Trio for fifteen years and now has a recording studio in St. Louis as well as doing many live performances.

Steve Davis, 2004. *Photograph by Dennis Owsley, with permission from Steve Davis.*

St. Louis has a New Orleans–style brass band, the Funky Butt Brass Band. They made four recordings in this period with their core members, Aaron Chandler (trombone), Adam Hucke (trumpet), Ben Reece or Austin Cebulske (saxophone), Matt Brinkmann (sousaphone), Tim Halpin (guitar) and Ron Sikes (percussion). The last two recordings had many guest performers [Discography].

Trumpeter Andy Tichenor is Trebor Tichenor's son. He is first-call trumpet for a lot of things, and he released an album of mostly Ellington material [Discography].

Two Webster University faculty members—pianist-composer Kim Portnoy and reed player–composer Paul DeMarinis—released CDs having to do with combining jazz with poetry. Portnoy's release uses the poetry of e.e. cummings as the basis for his original compositions and a jazz sextet with vocalists Debby Lennon, Charles Glen and Erin Bode, along with a jazz choir. DeMarinis writes both music and lyrics with Debby Lennon as part of the front line of a quintet [Discography]. This recording also features up-and-coming pianist Nick Schleuter, now a Webster faculty member.

In addition to Debby Lennon, there were other vocalists working. Mae Wheeler worked until she became ill and died in 2012. Jeanne Trevor continues to work sporadically. Ashley Mason made another recording with Steve Schenkel [Discography]. Christy John Bye works with Carolbeth True. Anita Jackson and Erika Johnson also seem to be working a lot. The author, Anita Jackson and the Two Times True group were involved in three music and photography multimedia concerts in this period.

Joe Mancuso[226] (born 1966) was born in St. Louis into a strong Italian family and was taken with the vocals of Frank Sinatra by the age of ten, when his aunt taught him guitar. After a degree in jazz and audio production from Webster University, he founded his own small recording studio. He gigged around St. Louis for a short time in 1996 and continued to work to support his family. In 2011, he went all in as a jazz vocalist and has never looked back. He made his only CD as a leader in 2013 and co-led a recording with guitarist Dave Black in 2016 [Discography].

Jan Shapiro, who was born in St. Louis, left to go on the road singing and playing in piano bars for ten years. She then became an academic vocal teacher and ended up as chair of the jazz vocal department at Berklee College of Music until 2010. She retired in 2017 and now lives in St. Louis.[227] Jan has recorded twice in Boston and has written a book, So You Want to Sing Jazz, published by Rowman/Littlefield.

A St. Louis native, Feyza Eren[228] spent fifteen years in Istanbul, Turkey, working as a jazz singer. Before she went to Turkey in 1995, she earned a

Joe Mancuso (*left*) and Willem von Hombracht. *Courtesy Joe Mancuso, with permission from Joe Mancuso and Willem von Hombracht.*

degree in broadcast journalism but then became a professional musician. She returned in 2011 and has worked extensively since. She made four recordings in Turkey and has made three since returning to St. Louis [*Discography*].

St. Louis vocalist Brian Owens has, until 2012, been on the fence between jazz music and rhythm and blues–soul music. Brian was born in Belleville and has appeared on CDs with Peter Martin and the Funky Butt Brass Band [*Discography*]. In a *Post-Dispatch* interview (March 2, 2012), Owens stated that he was returning to singing soul music. He is on the Webster University music faculty.

Brett Stamps headed up a five-trombone group that included himself with Cody Henry, Jim Owens and Dave Stamps on trombone and Jim Martin on bass trombone. They made a 2010 recording [*Discography*].

Alto saxophonist Jason Swagler[229] has been a member of the jazz studies department at Southern Illinois University–Edwardsville since 2000. He is now the director. Swagler recorded twice as a leader. His first recording as a leader was with guitarist Eric Slaughter, bassist Nick Jost and drummer Marty Morrison (2012). He and pianist Adaron Jackson recorded as a duo (2014) [*Discography*]. Jackson is also on the faculty and has recorded with Anita Rosamond and Lamar Harris and is a member of Good 4 the Soul.

Willie Akins and Montez Coleman recorded a CD with Peter Schlamb (vibes), Tony Suggs (piano), Eric Slaughter and Bob DeBoo in 2012. Willie

Zeb Brisovich (*left*) and Jason Swagler, 2015. *Photograph by Dennis Owsley, with permission from Zeb Briskovich and Jason Swagler.*

also recorded with Ray Kennedy (2000) and Prince Wells (2002) [*Discography*]. He was on the Webster University faculty and died in 2015. An annual Willie Akins Jazz Festival takes place at the Grandel Theater. Joe Mancuso set up a GoFundMe account page to help Willie and his family during his final illness.

The Bosman Twins recorded their first CD in 2014 with Ptah Williams, Eric Slaughter, Montez Coleman, Jeff Anderson, guitarist Darrel Darden and vocalist Cheryl D.S. Walker. The pianist on that date, Ptah Williams, made his first recordings as a leader in 2012 and 2015 for Autumn Hill Jazz [*all Discography*].

Saxophonist-composer-teacher Christopher Braig is a Webster University graduate and served as an adjunct faculty member (2005–16) and on the faculty of St. Louis Community College at Meramec. Paul DeMarinis said, "He can get music out of anybody"[230] through his innovative methods. Braig also travels a lot and has recorded a CD, playing all the instruments [*Discography*]. His teaching website offers lessons in brain training in music.[231]

Tenor saxophonist Larry Johnson continued recording with Jim Manley (2010, 2011). He made a recording with vocalist Michael Terry (2010) and Two Times True (2018). He made two recordings as a leader in 2009 and 2011 [*Discography*]. He continues to be an important member of Two Times True.

Carolbeth True and Larry Johnson, 2014.
Photograph by Dennis Owsley, with permission from Carolbeth True and Larry Johnson.

Smooth jazz saxophonist Tim Cunningham recorded two CDs during this period in 2012 and 2013 [*Discography*].

Pianist Ken Kehner[232] and his trio recorded at the Sheldon (2011). Kehner is a faculty member in the University of Missouri jazz studies department.

Keyboardist Ryan Marquez[233] recorded twice with drummer Steve Davis (2015 and 2018) and once with drummer Nick Slaughter (2018). Davis also led a trio with Nathan Jatko (2016). Carolbeth True's Two Times True group made a Christmas recording (2018), and Nick Schlueter recorded a CD with guitarist Brian Vaccaro and drummer Kyle Honeycutt in 2011. Vaccaro also recorded a CD in Edwardsville, Illinois, in 2000 [*Discography*].

Trumpeter-vocalist Dawn Weber[234] is a North Carolina native. The trumpet took her at age eleven. She went to the Winston-Salem Performing Arts High School and the Cleveland Conservatory and has won many awards. Dawn moved to St. Louis in 1998, played for Susan Slaughter and became a substitute for the symphony. Joining Vargas Swing, she eventually fronted the band and toured with it. She plays in many styles with many bands and recorded a jazz album in 2017 [*Discography*].

Guitarist-composer Dan Rubright[235] recorded three CDs in this period: a 2008 Christmas recording with vocalist Lydia Ruffin; a 2016 recording with his group, the Wire Pilots; and a 2018 recording with the Dan Rubright Group with Nick Schleuter [*all Discography*].

Ric Vice (*left*) and Dan Rubright, 2014. *Photograph by Dennis Owsley, with permission from Ric Vice and Dan Rubright.*

Avant-garde jazz and music related to jazz is often heard in concerts by the New Music Circle, which brings in various artists each year. James Hegarty, Principia College music chair and avant-garde jazz pianist and composer, and Joshua Weinstien, KDHX DJ, are on the board. Fred Tompkins is very active in the group.

The 2009–18 period has seen a quiet resurgence of avant-garde jazz. Tom Hamilton (electronics) recorded a group with trombonist James Martin at Webster University in 2009. Fred Tompkins made recordings in 2012 and 2016 [*all Discography*].

Jay Zelinka's company, Freedonia Music, issued nine recordings in this period. The core personnel on most of these recordings are Dave Stone (saxophones and electronics), Jay Zelinka (alto sax, electronics), Jeremy Melsha (turntable, electronics), Tracy Andreotti (cello), Greg Mills (piano) and guest musicians. Two were recorded in 2008–09, and the other seven were recorded from 2015 to 2017.

The other avant-garde jazz group in St. Louis is the STL Free Jazz Collective,[236] which recorded three digital download albums in 2015, 2017 and 2018. The musicians in the collective are Michael Castro (poet, deceased December 23, 2018), James Hegarty (keyboards), Baba Mike Nelson (trumpet, flugelhorn, shells, percussion, vocal), Paul Steinbeck (bass), Gary Sykes (drums) and Jerome "Jay Dubz" Williams (alto sax). Their website also contains videos of some of their performances.

Since the ragtime and early blues period around the turn of the nineteenth century, St. Louis jazz musicians have been people of substance who served the community and the nation not only as musical innovators but also as teachers, promoters, community leaders, award winners and leaders, sometimes in spite of barriers that should not have been there. It is hoped that this book has put away the myths that hold progress back and will point the way toward a brighter future for all.

NOTES

Introduction

1. Ayn Shipton, *A New History of Jazz* (New York: Continuum, 2001).
2. Kimball "Cabbage" Dial, interview by Frank Driggs, May 5, 1986. Frank Driggs Archives, University of Missouri–Kansas City.
3. Dennis C. Owsley, "Two Myths in St. Louis Jazz," *St. Louis Magazine*, May 24, 2011, http://www.stlmag.com.
4. Tom Lord Discography, https://lordisco.com/tjd.
5. Ibid.

Chapter 1

6. Jones, *Tom Turpin*.
7. Berlin, *King of Ragtime*.
8. Ibid.
9. Lord Discography.
10. Jones, *Tom Turpin*.
11. Dennis C. Owsley, "St. Louis Jazz Pioneer Jesse Johnson," *St. Louis Magazine*, www.stlmag.com.
12. Charles E. Rose, "The American Federation of Musicians and Its Effect on Black Musicians in St. Louis in the Twentieth Century" (master's thesis, Southern Illinois University–Edwardsville, 1978), 8–14.

13. Reich and Gaines, *Jelly's Blues*, 44–45.
14. Gushee, *Pioneers of Jazz*, 129.
15. Jones, *Tom Turpin*.
16. Harry Dial, *All This Jazz About Jazz: The Autobiography of Harry Dial* (Chigwell, Essex, UK: Storyville Publications, 1978).
17. *St. Louis Globe-Democrat*, July 22, 1945.

Chapter 2

18. Blues World, "St. Louis Blues Musicians," http://www.bluesworld.com/OTHERPRE.html.
19. Stoddard, *Pops Foster*, 106–15.
20. Ibid.
21. Singleton Palmer, interview by Bob Rusch, *Cadence Magazine*, February 1987, 5.
22. Kenney, *Jazz on the River*, 63.
23. George T. Simon, *The Big Bands* (New York: Macmillan, 1971).
24. William Howland Kenney, "Just Before Miles: Jazz in St. Louis. 1926–1944," in *Miles Davis and American Culture*, ed. Gerald Early (St. Louis: Missouri Historical Society Press, 2001), 24–39.
25. Floyd Campbell, quoted in Dempsey Travis, *An Autobiography of Black Jazz* (Chicago: Urban Research Institute, 1983), 239–40.
26. *St. Louis Globe-Democrat*, July 22, 1945.
27. New Orleans Rhythm Kings and Jelly Roll Morton, Milestone MCD-47020-2.
28. Evans, Kiner and Trumbauer, *Tram*, 26–29.
29. *New York Times* (Obituary), March 1, 1934.
30. Jones, *Tom Turpin*.
31. Evans, Kiner and Trumbauer, *Tram*.
32. Frederic Ramsey Jr. and Charles Edward Smith, *Jazzmen* (New York: Harcourt, Brace & Company, 1939); Red Hot Jazz, http://www.redhotjazz.com/mound.html.
33. Hilbert, *Pee Wee Russell*.
34. Dial, *All This Jazz about Jazz*.
35. Jones, *Tom Turpin*.
36. The information on these players was compiled from Dial, *All This Jazz about Jazz*.
37. Jones, *Tom Turpin*.

38. Ibid.

39. Ibid.

40. Scott Yanow, "Jerome Pasquall," All Music Guide, http://www.allmusic.com.

41. Jones, *Tom Turpin*.

42. Ibid.

43. Frank Driggs, *The New Grove Dictionary of Jazz*, ed. Barry Kernfield (New York: St. Martin's Press, 1995), 1200.

44. Kenney, "Just Before Miles."

45. Compiled from a private letter from Dan Vernhettes, Paris, France.

46. Kimball "Cabbage" Dial, interview by Frank Driggs, May 5, 1986, Frank Driggs Archives, University of Missouri–Kansas City.

47. Vertna Saunders, interview with Dan Havens, April 5, 1982, National Ragtime and Jazz Archive, Southern Illinois University–Edwardsville.

48. Paul DeMarinis, private communication.

49. Jean-Francois Pitet, "William Thornton Blue: The Creative but Forgotten Clarinetist," 2012, http://www.thehidehoblog.com/blog/2012/09/william-thornton-blue-the-creative-but-forgotten-clarinettist.

50. Mrs. William Rollins, interviewed by Frank Driggs, Charlie Menees and Jeff Leopold, September 28, 1978, Frank Driggs Archives, University of Missouri–Kansas City.

51. Kimball "Cabbage" Dial, Sammy Long and Elijah "Lige" Shaw, interviewed with Frank Driggs, September 24, 1978, Frank Driggs Archives, University of Missouri–Kansas City.

52. Dial, *All This Jazz about Jazz*.

53. Cunningham and Jones, *Sweet, Hot and Blue*, 73.

54. Dial, Long and Shaw, interview.

55. Dial, *All This Jazz about Jazz*.

56. Stoddard, *Pops Foster*.

57. Martin Williams, *Jazz Masters of New Orleans* (New York: Da Capo Press, 1979), 186.

Chapter 3

58. Pimm, *Lion of the Valley*, 467–72.

59. The information in this section was compiled from Rose, "American Federation of Musicians."

60. Ibid.

61. Dial, interview by Driggs, May 5, 1986.
62. Compiled from Hayes Pillars, interview by Frank Driggs, Frank Driggs Archives, University of Missouri–Kansas City, unknown date; Harry "Sweets" Edison, conversation with the author, Denver, Colorado, 1986; Hayes Pillars, interview by Wil Warner for Frank Driggs, Frank Driggs Archives, University of Missouri–Kansas City, unknown date.
63. Dial, interview by Driggs, May 5, 1986.
64. Leon King, interview by Dan Havens, August 1981, National Ragtime and Jazz Archive, Southern Illinois University–Edwardsville.
65. Dial, Long and Shaw, interview with Driggs, September 24, 1978.
66. Compiled from Druie Bess interview, conducted by Irene Cortinovis and Peter Etzkorn, November 5, 1971, Western Historical Manuscript Collection, University of Missouri–St. Louis, T-033; Eddie Randle, interview with the author; Eugene Chadbourne, "Druie Bess," All Music Guide, http://www.allmusic.com.
67. Stanley Dance, *The World of Duke Ellington* (New York: Da Capo Press, 2nd ed., 1970), 164–68.
68. Frank Driggs, "Don Stovall," *New Grove Dictionary of Jazz*, 1164–65.
69. *New Grove Dictionary of Jazz*, 1137–38.
70. Tom Lord, *Charlie Christian*, Discography.
71. Eugene Chadborn, "Karl George," All Music Guide, www.allmusic.com.
72. Jones, *Tom Turpin*.
73. Cunningham and Jones, *Sweet, Hot and Blue*, 35–36.
74. Compiled from Frank Driggs, "Tab Smith," *New Grove Dictionary of Jazz*, 1142–43; Ian Carr, Digby Fairweather and Brian Priestley, *Jazz: The Essential Companion* (New York: Prentice Hall, 1987), 465.
75. American Big Bands Database, http://nfo.net/usa/j1.html.
76. Owsley, *City of Gabriels*, 75–80.
77. Jones, *Tom Turpin*.

Chapter 4

78. John Cotter, "The Negro in Music in St. Louis," master's thesis, Washington University, St. Louis, Missouri, 1959, 461–62.
79. Lloyd Smith interview from *Lift Every Voice and Sing*, ed. Wesley, Price and Morris, 75.
80. Robert Carter interview from *Lift Every Voice and Sing*, 24.
81. Pillars, interview by Driggs.

82. Cotter, "The Negro in Music in St. Louis," 342–45.
83. Ibid.
84. Davis, *Miles*, 14–15, 28–29.
85. Bobby Danzig, interview by Charles Rose, National Ragtime and Jazz Archive, Southern Illinois University–Edwardsville.
86. Carr, *Miles Davis*, 14.
87. Dizzy Gillespie with Al Fraser, *To Be or Not…to Bop* (New York: Doubleday, 1979), 188; Art Blakey, quoted in Robert Riesner, *Bird: The Legend of Charlie Parker* (New York: Da Capo Press, 1975), 51.
88. Pillars, interview by Driggs.
89. Davis, *Miles*, 45.
90. Billy Eckstine, *Melody Maker*, September 4, 1954.
91. The key recordings that instituted these changes were *The Birth of the Cool* (Capitol, 1950), *Kind of Blue* (Columbia, 1959), *Miles Smiles* (Columbia, 1966) and *Bitches Brew* (Columbia, 1970).
92. Compiled mainly from Schacter, *Piano Man*.
93. Adapted from Peter Vacher, "Jimmy Forrest," *New Grove Dictionary of Jazz*, 400.
94. *St. Louis Argus*, all issues from 1946 to year-end 1950.
95. Cotter, "The Negro in Music in St. Louis," 358–59 and 460–63.
96. "Biography of Louis Daniel Armstrong," Louis Armstrong Educational Foundation, LouisArmstrongFoundation.org.
97. *New Grove Dictionary of Jazz*, 771.
98. Johnny Simmen, "Arvell Shaw," *New Grove Dictionary of Jazz*, 1108.

Chapter 5

99. Adapted from Vacher, "Jimmy Forrest," *New Grove Dictionary of Jazz*, 400.
100. Steve Voce, "Obituary: Ernie Wilkins," https://independent.co.uk/arts-entertainment/obituary-ernie-wilkins-1098835.html.
101. Marc Myers, "Jimmy Wilkins (1921–2018)," Jazz Wax, https://www.jazzwax.com/2018/08/jimmy-wilkins-1921-2018.html.
102. Robert L. Campbell, Armin Büttner and Robert Pruter, "Tommy Dean Discography," http://hubcap.clemson.edu/~campber/deanie.html.
103. Peter Vacher, "Chris Woods," *New Grove Dictionary of Jazz*, 1306.
104. Barry Kernfeld, "Oliver Nelson," *New Grove Dictionary of Jazz*, 833–34.

105. Irene Cortinovis, interview with Eddie Johnson, Elijah Shaw, Chick Finney and Eddie Randle, August 20, 1971, University of Missouri, St. Louis Historical Manuscript Collection No. T-010.

106. Ibid.

107. Dennis Owsley, "Two Myths of St. Louis Jazz," *St. Louis Magazine*, May 24, 2011, https://www.stlmag.com/culture/Two-Myths-of-St-Louis-Jazz.

108. Sandra Pointer Jones, "Delmark History," from an article in *Blues Revue Quarterly*, http://delmark.com/delmark.history.htm.

109. KETC, "Herb Drury," *Living St. Louis*, https://www.youtube.com/watch?v=j4rhecXTrpU.

110. CTS Images, "Bernie Thrasher," http://ctsimages.com/pages/archives/thrasher_bernie.html.

111. Alex Henderson, "Bob Graf," All Music Guide, http://www.allmusic.com.

112. Jones, *Tom Turpin*.

113. Green, *Grant Green*.

114. *St. Louis Argus*, June 6, 1953.

115. Inside Jazz, "Hugh 'Peanuts' Whalum," https://insidejazz.com/2018/01/hugh-peanuts-whalum.

116. Lee Hyde, interview with Dennis Owsley and Jim Wallace, *Jazz Spectrum*, KWMU, St. Louis, 1985.

117. Lee Hyde, interview with the author, March 24, 1986.

118. S. Duncan Reid, *Cal Tjader: The Life and Recordings of the Man Who Revolutionized Latin Jazz* (Jefferson, NC: McFarland, 2013).

119. Leonard Feather and Ira Gitler, *The Encyclopedia of Jazz in the Seventies* (New York: Horizon Press, 1976).

120. Robert Spencer, "Buddy Childers Biography," All about Jazz, http://www.allaboutjazz.com/artists/bchilders.htm.

121. *New Grove Dictionary of Jazz*, "Bob Gordon," 441.

122. Lee Jeske, "Leon Thomas," *New Grove Dictionary of Jazz*, 1201.

Chapter 6

123. Kenny Rice, quoted in Green, *Grant Green*, 75.

124. Cunningham and Jones, *Sweet, Hot and Blue*, 206–08.

125. Crone, *Gaslight Square*.

'6. Ibid.

127. *St. Louis Post-Dispatch*, "Sammy Gardner" (Obituary), June 25, 1995.

128. Crone, *Gaslight Square*, 60.

129. *St. Louis Post-Dispatch*, "Ceil Clayton" (Obituary), June 25, 1997.
130. Compiled mainly from a Clea Bradford publicity brochure, courtesy of Al Becker.
131. Leonard Feather, *Encyclopedia of Jazz in the Sixties* (New York: Da Capo 1986), 66.
132. Crone, *Gaslight Square*, 56–68.
133. Ibid.
134. Henry Ettman, telephone conversation with the author, February 1, 2006.
135. Crone, *Gaslight Square*.
136. Boogie Woogie Press, "Rent Party Echoes: The Role of the Louisville, Dallas, Fort Worth, Evansville Piano Parties in the History of Boogie Woogie Piano—As Seen by Charlie Booty," https://www.colindavey. com/boogiewoogie/articles/booty.htm.
137. Austin Belmear, private communication with the author, 2018.
138. Ibid.

Chapter 7

139. Compiled from correspondence from Eddie Fisher with the author, 2003.
140. Compiled from Cunningham and Jones, *Sweet, Hot and Blue*, 118–22.
141. Compiled from information on Carolbeth True's website, http:// carolbethtrue.com.
142. Compiled from Lester Bowie, interview with Jim Wallace; Lester Bowie, interview with Bob Rusch; Lee Jeske, "Lester Bowie," *New Grove Dictionary of Jazz*, 140–41.
143. Compiled from Oliver Lake, interview with Bob Rusch; Barry Kernfield, "Oliver Lake," *New Grove Dictionary of Jazz*, 673; Oliver Lake website, http://www.oliverlake.net; The European Jazz Network, http:// www.ejn.it/mus/lake.htm.
144. J.D. Parran, press release, December 2005.
145. This information excerpted and compiled from Baikida Carroll's website, http://www.baikida.com/bio2.html.
146. Looker, *Point from Which Creation Begins*, 31.
147. Compiled from information from Subito Music, http://w subitomusic.com/hemphill_bio.htm.
148. Chris Kelsey, "Hamiet Bluiett," All Music Guide, http://allmusic.com.

149. Looker, *Point from Which Creation Begins*, 70.

150. Ro Burrage Production, http://ronnieburrage.biz.

151. Compiled from an interview on the Omnitone Records website, http://www.omnitone.com/malinkesdance/ehrlich-interview.htm; Marty Ehrlich, http://www.martyehrlich.com/marty.html.

152. Looker, *Point from Which Creation Begins*, 89–90.

153. Compiled from Carol Loewenstein, interview by Benjamin Looker, November 6, 2003; James Marshall, interview by Benjamin Looker, August 11, 2003, in Looker, "Interviews on the Black Artists' Group (BAG) of St. Louis," unpublished collection, 2004, held at Special Collections, Washington University in St. Louis.

154. Dylan Hassinger, "A Brief History of the Double Helix," ProgressiveSTL.com. http://www.progressivestl.com/?p 62.

155. Malinke Elliot, private conversation with the author, BAG Symposium at Washington University, February 2, 2006.

156. Looker, *Point from Which Creation Begins*, 190–91.

157. Rose, "American Federation of Musicians."

158. Wikipedia, "Ray Kennedy," https://en.wikipedia.org/wiki/Ray_Kennedy_(pianist).

159. http://www.gregosby.com biography and interviews.

160. St. Louis Media History, http://www.stlmediahistory.com/Radio/Personalities, covers the names and dates of the jazz radio personalities listed in this chapter.

Chapter 8

161. http://www.archcitydefenders.org/wp-content/uploads/2014/11/ArchCity-Defenders-Municipal-Courts-Whitepaper.pdf; https://www.stlmag.com/news/the-color-line-race-in-st.-louis; https://forthesakeofall.org/wpcontent/uploads/2018/04/SegregationinSTL_DismantlingDivideReport.pdf.

162. Rose, "American Federation of Musicians."

163. "Dave Weckl," Wikipedia, https://en.wikipedia.org/wiki/Dave_Weckl.

164. Jay Oliver, http://www.jayoliver.com.

165. Kent Miller Quartet, http://katesmithpromotions.com/artists/KentMillerQuartet.html.

166. Peter Martin, http://www.petermartinmusic.com.

167. "Biography," Neal Caine, http://beta.asoundstrategy.com/sitemaster/useruploads/site157/neal_caine_press_kit.pdf.

168. "Bio," Chris Cheek, http://www.chrischeek.net/Bio.html.

169. Terry Perkins, "After 46 Years of Playing Together, Bosman Twins Look to Something New: Record," St. Louis Public Radio, http://news.stlpublicradio.org/post/after-46-years-playing-together-bosman-twins-look-something-new-record#stream/0.

170. "Reginald Thomas," MRT Jazz, http://mrtjazz.com/?page_id=174.

171. "Russell Gunn," All Music Guide, https://www.allmusic.com/artist/russell-gunn-mn0000180614/biography.

172. Terreon Gully, https://terreongully.com.

173. "Montez Coleman," All Music Guide, https://www.allmusic.com/artist/montez-coleman-mn0000140988/credits.

174. "Tony Suggs," All Music Guide, https://www.allmusic.com/artist/tony-suggs-mn0000718524.

175. "Andre Roberson," All Music Guide, https://www.allmusic.com/artist/andre-roberson-mn0002340487.

176. "Bruce Purse," All Music Guide, https://www.allmusic.com/artist/bruce-purse-mn0000940440/credits.

177. "Bio," Eric Person, http://ericperson.com/bio.

178. Thomas Crone, Terry Perkins and Steve Pick, "Listening Post," *Riverfront Times*, February 10, 1999, https://www.riverfronttimes.com/stlouis/listening-post/Content?oid=2481389.

179. "Parker," My St. Louis, http://stlouishistory.blogspot.com/2012/03/parker.html.

180. Eric Markowitz, http://www.ericmarkowitz.com/html/about.php.

181. "Dave Stone," Freedonia Music, http://freedoniamusic.org/catalog/fm23.html.

182. Eddie Randle, private conversation with the author.

183. Julius Hemphill, *Julius Hemphill Big Band*, Elektra Musician 9 60831-2 (1988).

Chapter 9

184. "The Wolff Jazz Institute," Harris-Stowe State University, www.hssu.edu/rsp_index.cfm?wid=42.

185. Jones, *Tom Turpin*.

186. Nu-Art Metro Gallery, https://www.youtube.com/user/NuArtMetroGallery.

187. Stephanie Trick, http://stephanietrick.com.

188. "Kim Portnoy," Webster University, http://www.webster.edu/music/faculty/portnoy-kim.html.

189. Lawrence Fields, https://www.lawrencefields.com.

190. "Steve Schenkel," Webster University, http://www.webster.edu/music/faculty/schenkel-steve.html.

191. "Rob Block," Mezzrow, https://www.mezzrow.com/artists/2446-rob-block.

192. Dave Black, https://www.daveblackstl.com/bio.

193. "Tom Byrne," Webster University, http://www.webster.edu/music/faculty/byrne-tom.html.

194. "Rick Haydon," Southern Illinois University–Edwardsville, https://www.siue.edu/artsandsciences/music/faculty/Haydon.shtml.

195. "William Lenihan," Washington University in St. Louis, https://music.wustl.edu/people/william-lenihan.

196. "Willem von Hombracht," Webster University, http://www.webster.edu/music/faculty/hombracht-willem-von.html.

197. Denise Thimes, https://denisethimes.com/about.

198. Kevin Johnson, "Mae Wheeler Dies; St. Louis Jazz Singer," *St. Louis Post-Dispatch*, June 17, 2011, https://www.stltoday.com/news/local/obituaries/mae-wheeler-dies-st-louis-jazz-singer/article_2260d1fb-8e4b-55c4-9fe7-4cbec09f353b.html.

199. John Becker, private conversation with the author.

200. Valerie Tichacek, http://www.valerietichacek.com.

201. "Reginald Thomas." MRT Jazz.

202. "Debby Lennon," Webster University, http://www.webster.edu/music/faculty/lennon-debby.html.

203. Cunningham and Jones, *Sweet, Hot & Blue*.

204. All About Jazz, "Michael Parkinson," https://musicians.allaboutjazz.com/michaelparkinson.

205. Prince A. Wells III, https://www.princewells.com/prince-wells-bio.html.

206. "Jeremy Clemons," Dream Cymbals, https://dreamcymbals.com/artists/usa/clemons-jeremy.

207. Keyon Harrold, https://www.keyonharrold.com.

208. "Brett Stamps," Trombone Page of the World, http://www.trombone-usa.com/stamps_brett_bio.htm.

209. "James A. Martin," Webster University, http://www.webster.edu/music/faculty/martin-james.html.

210. "Jim Owens," Gateway City Big Band, http://www.gatewaycitybigband.com/director.html.

211. "Paul DeMarinis," Webster University, http://www.webster.edu/music/faculty/demarinis-paul.html.

212. Fred Tompkins, http://tompkinsjazz.com/st-louis/biography.php.

213. Roscoe Crenshaw, "Remembering John Norment, Jazz Saxaphonist," *St. Louis American*, http://www.stlamerican.com/entertainment/living_it/remembering-john-norment-jazz-saxophonist/article_b4f3cd66-a3b0-563b-ada1-90837304f43d.html.

214. "Kevin Gianino," Webster University, http://www.webster.edu/music/faculty/gianino-kevin.html.

215. "Kimberly Thompson," Audix Microphones, https://audixusa.com/cgi-bin/adx_coranto2/viewnews.cgi?id=EuyZZyupuuxYwtqVwY&style=user_story&tmpl=artist_1.

216. Jones, *Tom Turpin*.

217. Late Bloomer, http://www.doubleberg.com.

218. "Jim Orso," Sabian, https://sabian.com/en/artist/jim-orso.

219. Emanuel Harrold, https://www.therealemanuelharrold.com/about-e.

220. "Miles Vandiver," Southern Illinois University–Edwardsville, https://www.siue.edu/artsandsciences/music/faculty/Vandiver.shtml.

221. Ron Wynn, "Where's the Black Audience?" *Jazz Times*, January 1, 2003, https://jazztimes.com/features/wheres-the-black-audience.

Chapter 10

222. Jazz St. Louis, https://jazzstl.org.

223. Jacques Steinberg, "Pulitzer to Be Acquired by Lee Enterprises," *New York Times*, https://www.nytimes.com/2005/02/01/business/media/pulitzer-to-be-acquired-by-lee-enterprises.html.

224. Dennis Owsley, "Will the Big Bands Ever Come Back?" *St. Louis Magazine*, https://www.stlmag.com/culture/Will-the-Big-Bands-Ever-Come-Back.

225. Steve Davis Drums, http://www.stevedavisdrums.com.

226. Joe Mancuso, http://mancusojazz.com/press-kit/joe-mancuso-short-bio.

227. "Jan Shapiro," All Music Guide, https://www.allmusic.com/artist/jan-shapiro-mn0000709374/biography.

228. Feyza Eren, https://www.feyzaeren.com/bio.

229. "Jason Swagler," Southern Illinois University–Edwardsville, https://www.siue.edu/artsandsciences/music/faculty/Swagler.shtml.

230. Nassim Benchaabane, "Saxophonist Combines Innovative Performance and Teaching to Sustain Personal and Professional Life," St. Louis Public Radio, http://news.stlpublicradio.org/post/saxophonist-combines-innovative-performance-and-teaching-sustain-personal-and-professional-life#stream/0.

231. Jazz Brain Training, https://jazzbraintraining.teachable.com.

232. "Ken Kehner," University of Missouri–St. Louis, https://music.umsl.edu/Faculty/KenKehner.html.

233. Ryan Marquez, http://www.ryanmarquez.com/about.

234. Dawn Weber, http://dawnweber.com/home/bio.

235. Dan Rubright, http://www.danrubrightmusic.com/about.html.

236. STL Free Jazz Collective, http://www.stlfreejazz.com.

BIBLIOGRAPHY

Berlin, Edward A. *King of Ragtime: Scott Joplin and His Era*. New York: Oxford University Press, 1996.

Carr, Ian. *Miles Davis: The Definitive Biography*. New York: Thunder Mouth Press, 1998.

Crone, Thomas. *Gaslight Square: An Oral History*. St. Louis, MO: William and Joseph Press, 2004.

Cunningham, Lynn Driggs, and Jimmy Jones. *Sweet, Hot and Blue: St. Louis Musical Heritage*. Jefferson, NC: McFarland, 1989.

Davis, Miles, with Quincy Troupe. *Miles: The Autobiography*. New York: Simon and Schuster, 1989.

Evans, Philip R., Larry F. Kiner and William Trumbauer. *Tram: The Frank Trumbauer Story*. Metuchen, NJ: Scarecrow Press, 1994.

Green, Sharony Andrews. *Grant Green: Rediscovering the Forgotten Genius of Jazz Guitar*. New York: Backbeat Books, 2002.

Gushee, Lawrence. *Pioneers of Jazz: The Story of the Creole Band*. New York: Oxford University Press, 2005.

Hilbert, Robert. *Pee Wee Russell: The Life of a Jazzman*. New York: Oxford University Press, 1993.

Jones, Gordon G. *Tom Turpin: His Life and Music*. The Tom Turpin Ragtime Festival, 1995.

Kenney, William Howland. *Jazz on the River*. Chicago: University of Chicago Press, 2005.

BIBLIOGRAPHY

Looker, Benjamin. *Point from Which Creation Begins*. St. Louis: Missouri Historical Society Press, 2004.

Owsley, Dennis C. *City of Gabriels: The Jazz History of St. Louis, 1895–1973*. St. Louis, MO: Reedy Press, 2006.

Pimm, James. *Lion of the Valley*. Boulder, CO: Pruett Publishing, 1981.

Reich, Howard, and William Gaines. *Jelly's Blues*. Cambridge, MA: Da Capo Press, 2003.

Schacter, James D. *Piano Man: The Story of Ralph Sutton*. Chicago: Jaynar Press, 1975.

Stoddard, Tom. *Pops Foster: The Autobiography of a New Orleans Jazzman*. Berkeley: University of California Press, 1971.

Wesley, Doris A., Wiley Price and Ann Morris, eds. *Lift Every Voice and Sing: St. Louis African Americans in the Twentieth Century*. Columbia: University of Missouri Press, 1999.

INDEX

ABOUT THE AUTHOR

Dennis Owsley was born near Los Angeles, California, and earned a BA in chemistry and a PhD in organic chemistry from the University of California in Riverside. He and his late wife, Rosa, came to St. Louis in 1969 for Dennis to take a job with Monsanto. He retired in 1996 as one of the top scientists in that corporation. He also taught chemistry at the college and university levels in 1978–83 and 1996–2001.

He has been a jazz album collector, aficionado and historian since 1958 and has seen most of the major artists in jazz in live performance. April 2019 marked his thirty-sixth anniversary presenting jazz on St. Louis Public Radio. He celebrated his twenty-fifth anniversary with a mayoral proclamation of a Dennis Owsley Day on January 24, 2008. He received the Millard S. Cohen Lifetime Achievement Award from St. Louis Public Radio in 2010 and was named a Jazz Hero of St. Louis by the Jazz Journalists Association. *Jazz Unlimited* won the *Riverfront Times* Best of St. Louis Award in the "Best Jazz Show" category six times. He produced *The Jazz History of St. Louis* on St. Louis Public Radio, the second-longest music documentary in the history of radio, in 2014.

A noted jazz photographer, he had his own show, "In the Moment," at the Sheldon Art Gallery in 2005, and his images were part of two other shows in that gallery. His photographs have appeared on websites all over the world, on album covers and in various other media. In 2006, he published an award-winning book, *City of Gabriels: The Jazz History of St. Louis, 1895–1973*. That same year, he co-curated the exhibit "The Jazz History of St. Louis." This exhibit was mounted again in 2013.